In Se ---
of
Freedom

The Pilgrim Fathers and New England

J. R. BROOME

2001

GOSPEL STANDARD TRUST PUBLICATIONS
12(b) Roundwood Lane, Harpenden, Herts.
AL5 3DD, England

ISBN: 1 897837 32 1

Published by:
Gospel Standard Trust Publications

Cover picture :
Sunset at Land's End, Cornwall

Printed and bound in Great Britain by
The Cromwell Press
Aintree Avenue, White Horse Business Park,
Trowbridge, Wilts, BA14 OXB

Contents

CHAPTER 1

The Church of Christ

The early Separatists

When the Pilgrim Fathers sailed from Southampton on the 5th August, 1620, and after some delay finally left their home country from the port of Plymouth on the 6th September, a long history lay behind them in their own country of persecution for the truth's sake. It would seem strange that they should disagree with the Protestant Church of Queen Elizabeth, whose doctrines were based upon the "Thirty nine Articles", but it was not disagreement with these "Articles" which led them to leave the shores of their native land. Their disagreement was with a National Church, especially one based upon a parish system which admitted all and sundry, baptised and confirmed, to the Lord's Table. They would have agreed with John Wycliffe when he said, "The temple of God is the congregation ... of just men for whom Jesus shed His blood." Wycliffe died in 1384.

In 1401 the first Act of Parliament was passed for the burning of heretics, and in the next sixty-five years over one hundred and twenty people were tried under this Act for heresy. Prior to the Act of Supremacy (1544), which severed the Church of England from Rome, Foxe (the author of the *Book of Martyrs*) tells us that there "were secret multitudes who tasted and followed the sweetness of God's Holy Word". Even in the reign of Edward VI (1547-1553), as the Reformation advanced, the Privy Council examined a private assembly of about sixty people who met in their own homes on Sunday, and separated themselves from the Anglican Church, and had not been to Communion at the Parish Church for over two years. The Privy Council saw fit to arrest at least sixteen of these people. In the reign of Queen Mary, which began in 1553, large groups of these Separatists met at night in secret gatherings, moving from house to house to avoid detection. London itself had such a Church, which appears to have continued its existence into the reign of Queen Elizabeth. Foxe refers to this Church, which he says at first numbered about forty, and then rose to two hundred. William Bradford, one of the leaders of the Pilgrim Fathers, writes about this congregation and says, "In the days of Queen Elizabeth there was a separated Church (in London) whereof Mr. Fitz was pastor, and another before that in the time of Queen Mary (1553-1558), of which Mr. Rough was pastor ." In 1557 this congregation was detected and John Rough was burnt at Smithfield ten days after his arrest, and the deacon of the Church,

Cuthbert Symson, was burnt in the same place on the 28th March, 1558. This Church continued more openly in existence in the reign of Queen Elizabeth, but was not entirely free from persecution. In 1571, giving their address as Whitechapel Street, London, twenty-seven members signed a petition to Queen Elizabeth, which read, "We, a poor congregation, whom God hath separated from the Church of England, and from the mingled and false worshipping therein . . . as God giveth strength at this day, do serve the Lord every Sabbath day in houses, and on the fourth day come together weekly to use prayer, and exercise discipline on them that do deserve it, by the strength and true warrant of the Lord God's word."

There is no doubt that in the reign of Elizabeth large numbers of the ministers in the Anglican Church were the same men who had celebrated Mass in the times of Mary, and had probably maintained their positions in the reigns of Edward VI and Henry VIII. As religious worldly men they moved with the times. When Grindal moved from being Bishop of London to become Archbishop of York in 1570, he found his northern diocese full of many superstitious Roman Catholic practices. Even in the south things were not much better. In the diocese of Chichester in 1569 there were churches which had not heard a sermon for seven years, and in the deanery of Midhurst there were clergymen who had preached in the reign of Queen Mary, and who had kept their parishes in the reign of Elizabeth, but had refused to preach since the death of Mary in 1558. It was in such a time and in such conditions that many godly men bore witness to a revelation of truth and church order, which they held to be more scriptural than that of the National Church. They were called 'Separatists' or 'Congregationalists', and in the reign of Elizabeth they stood out principally in three localities, East Anglia, London, and the churches at Scrooby in Nottinghamshire and Gainsborough in Lincolnshire, from which the Pilgrim Fathers came.

The leader of the Congregationalists in East Anglia was Robert Browne. In the reign of Elizabeth men who believed as he did were frequently called Brownists. As a Separatist Browne was persecuted by the Government of Elizabeth and during his lifetime went to prison at least thirty times. He was a Cambridge graduate, having obtained his degree in 1572. Between 1582 and 1584 he published five books on separation from the Church of England. He travelled about the country spreading his beliefs, especially in such cities as Norwich and Bury St. Edmunds, and then eventually with some of his supporters left the country and went to Holland in 1583, where they established a Congregational Church in Middleburg in Zealand. But it appears about 1586 he returned to England and joined the Church of England, in whose midst he remained until his death. While his name is thus used to refer to 'Congregational' or 'Separatist' congregations, it is clear that there were many who preceded him holding the same beliefs, and many who consistently maintained that Separatist position after he had returned to the Church of England.

In 1581 an Act was passed imposing a fine of £20 a month on all who refused to attend the Church of England. At Bury St. Edmunds in June 1583 Elias Thacker and John Copping were tried before the Lord Chief Justice in the Assizes, were condemned to death for distributing the books of Robert Browne, and were hung within a day of their conviction. In October 1587, John Greenwood, a graduate of Cambridge University (1581), and formerly a minister of the Church of England until 1585, was arrested with twenty others at a secret meeting of Separatists in London. After examination before the Bishop of London he was sent to the Clink Prison. While there he was visited by Henry Barrow, the son of a country squire of Shipdam in Norfolk. This young man had been trained for the Law in London, and had led an utterly godless life as a student, but passing a London church, he had turned in to hear the preacher, and the ministry had been so blessed to him that his life had been completely changed.

Now he was not ashamed to visit his friend John Greenwood in prison, but no sooner had he entered the prison than he was arrested himself, and having been examined by the Archbishop of Canterbury and his officials, he and Greenwood were given a room together in the Fleet Prison. Here the years passed slowly while they spent their time writing books vindicating their principles of separation from the Established Church. After five years, in 1592

Greenwood was released for a short while, but was re-arrested on December 5th, and on the 23rd March, 1593 Barrow and Greenwood were brought to trial at the Old Bailey for writing seditious books. After one reprieve by Queen Elizabeth they were taken to Tyburn and executed on the 6th April, 1593. They had made their stand for the very principle which drove the Pilgrim Fathers from their home country, first to Holland and then across the Atlantic to America.

William Bradford and William Brewster

Now we come to the group of Separatists who centred around the little village of Scrooby in Nottinghamshire, and who were scattered in the adjoining counties of Yorkshire and Lincolnshire. William Bradford in his writings has referred to the beginnings of the Separatist Church, and says that its members "were of several towns and villages, some in Nottinghamshire, some in Lincolnshire, and some in Yorkshire, where the counties bordered nearest together; they ordinarily met at William Brewster's house on the Lord's Day, which was a manor of the Bishop's." The home of William Brewster has now been established to have been at Scrooby, a mile and a half south of Bawtry, a market town within the Yorkshire border on the Great North Road from London to Berwick. It has also been established that William Bradford lived at Austerfield a mile or so to the north-east of Bawtry.

William Bradford was the chronicler of the Pilgrim Fathers in New England, and also an early governor of Plymouth Colony. His manuscript of things he could remember, jotted down over many years, is called *A History of Plymouth Plantation.* Various writers such as Nathaniel Morton in his *New England's Memorial* made use of it. In 1758 this manuscript was placed in the tower of the Old South Church in Boston, New England. During the American War of Independence, after the siege of Boston, the manuscript disappeared, and was presumed lost. It was not rediscovered until the middle of the nineteenth century, when it was found in 1855 in the library of the Bishop of London's Palace at Fulham. Presumably it had been brought to England by British soldiers after the withdrawal of the British Army from the American Colonies.

William Bradford and William Brewster were two noted leaders of the Pilgrim Fathers. The elder of the two men was Brewster, who was born about 1566 in the village of Scrooby. When he was about ten years old, his father was appointed bailiff of the Manor House at Scrooby by the Archbishop of York. His family also had a longstanding connection with Scrooby, his father having held the office of Master of the Posts, an office which passed to his widow in 1590 and was later confirmed to her son. It is also possible that young Brewster's grandfather had held this office before him, back in the earlier days of Queen Elizabeth.

After receiving his early education in some neighbouring school, William Brewster "spent some small time at Cambridge", where he matriculated at

Peterhouse on the 3rd December, 1580, at the age of fourteen. He did not stay there long enough to obtain a degree, but next appears in the service of William Davison, Queen Elizabeth I's representative to the Netherlands, whom he accompanied to that country in 1585. William Bradford in his *History of Plymouth Plantation* says of Brewster, "After being first seasoned with the seeds of grace and virtue, he went to the court, and served that religious and godly gentleman, William Davison, divers years when he was Secretary of State."

So we find William Brewster in the court of Queen Elizabeth, and to explain the possibilities of how this may have come about, we have to go back to the office of his father and grandfather as Master of the Posts at Scrooby. Until the reign of Henry VIII there was no regular system of posts in England, and long after that there were only four which were for the regular use of the Sovereign. The posts were always spoken of as journeys from the court, i.e. the court to Berwick (Scotland), the court to Beaumaris (Ireland), the court to Dover (the Continent), the court to Plymouth (the Royal Dockyard). Not only did the post convey the royal letters, but it provided a constant relay of horses along these four main roads of the kingdom, so that persons travelling on the affairs of State might move quickly from place to place. So to the Manor House of Scrooby on the Great North Road there came a constant stream of visitors, who put up for the night, and went on in the morning with their fresh horses.

Here it would appear William Brewster, in his own home, met Davison. In August, 1585, he accompanied him to the Netherlands, and when on his return Davison became assistant to Walsingham, the Queen's Secretary of State, from the autumn of 1586 to the following February Brewster was with him in the court at Richmond where Davison was in daily attendance upon the Queen. Not only was Davison a capable and honest statesman, he was also a godly man, and strangely, during his service in the Netherlands, he was an elder of the English Puritan refugee Church in Antwerp. The records of that Church speak of his eldership, and also record the birth of "divers children to Mr. William Davison, Ambassador of Queen Elizabeth in Antwerp".

It would seem that Davison treated Brewster more like a son than a servant, and we can begin to understand how Brewster developed desires for a larger measure of religious freedom, and also a love for the truth, as he daily attended his master, and mingled with the refugees in the Netherlands. Before him, it would appear, was a brilliant political future. But the Lord had other purposes for William Brewster, and the man who had spent his youth in the highest circles in the land was eventually to flee from his country as a refugee and become one of the Pilgrim Fathers.

The change in his career came about suddenly and unexpectedly, through no less an event than the execution of Knox's great opponent, Mary Queen of Scots. She was a prisoner at Fotheringay Castle just south of Stamford. She was in direct line of descent to Elizabeth, who had no children. As a Roman Catholic, she had connived at many plots to kill Queen Elizabeth, and finally the Queen had signed her death warrant, and handed it to Davison, who took it to Fotheringay where Mary Queen of Scots was executed on February 9th, 1587. When news of the execution reached Queen Elizabeth, she found it convenient to deny responsibility, and to make Davison the scapegoat, saying that whilst she had signed the death warrant, she had never ordered him to take it to Fotheringay. As a result, he was arrested, sent to the Tower, deprived of his Secretaryship, and heavily fined. For Brewster, this meant the end of his career at the court. Bradford says that towards the end of 1587, Brewster "went and lived in the country, in good esteem amongst his friends and the gentlemen of those parts, especially the godly and religious". In other words he went back to Scrooby.

He was now about twenty-one. His father was ailing, and died in the summer of 1590. After a short interval William was made Post of Scrooby, and continued to hold that important office for the next seventeen years, until he fled to Holland in 1607. In fact, the State papers and accounts of the time show that the last payment made to him for this office was for the period 1st April to the last day of September 1607, thus telling us precisely when William Brewster went into exile. These were formative years, and we hope later to attempt to trace out some of the influences which led William Brewster to prefer to "suffer affliction with the people of God" than to stay in his quiet Manor House at Scrooby and attend the Anglican Church there. One thing is clear, William Brewster came from a family of considerable standing among the lesser gentry of Queen Elizabeth, yet he did not shun, for the sake of the truth, to cast aside these worldly comforts into which he had been born, to go first to Holland and then America, with all the hazards that this entailed for him and his family.

With him also went William Bradford. He was his junior by some twenty-three years, and had been born at Austerfield, a village about three miles north of Scrooby. Between Scrooby and Austerfield lies the town of Bawtry. This is the area of the Yorkshire, Lincolnshire and Nottinghamshire borders. Just over thirty miles to the south lies Nottingham; thirty to forty miles to the north, York; thirty miles to the south-east Lincoln; and a further thirty miles to the south-east, Boston. Over forty miles away to the north-east lie Hull and Grimsby. We mention these details to establish the geographical setting of the countryside from which the Pilgrim Fathers came. Though Sheffield lay only fifteen miles to the west of them, on the eastern edge of the Pennines, their outlook was towards the sea and the lowlands of Lincolnshire lying between the Wash and the Humber. It was from this coastal region that they braved the dangers of the sea to cross to Holland. Today Bawtry, about eight miles south of Doncaster, is on the main northern line from King's Cross to Edinburgh. In the days of the Pilgrim Fathers it lay on the equally important road route from London to the north.

Bradford's father came from good English yeoman stock. He died when William was about a year old, leaving him in the care of his grandfather. When the boy was about six his grandfather died, and he was then brought up by his uncles. His family were farmers, and it seems clear that this was the work to which William devoted his early years. The yeoman class who followed husbandry came next to the acknowledged gentry. It would seem therefore that William Brewster and William Bradford were born into a similar social background, though Brewster had some advantages over his younger friend Bradford. It was as a young man of fifteen or sixteen years of age that William Bradford was brought into the company of William Brewster, and travelled with him on a Sunday the ten or twelve miles to the gathering of the first Separatist group which met in the town of Gainsborough (due east of Bawtry) in the year 1602. Here under the ministry of John Smyth, M.A., of Christ's College, Cambridge, they worshipped until a second group established a regular meeting at Scrooby in William Brewster's house. Thus the two men were brought together, one a lad of eighteen or twenty and the other a man of forty at the time when they left their country to go into exile.

The Separatists at Scrooby and Gainsborough

William Bradford in his *History of Plymouth Plantation* traces the rise of the Scrooby Church, of which he himself was a leading member, to the effects of the ministry of various Puritan clergymen who were ministers of Anglican Churches in the vicinity. He says, "By the travail and diligence of some godly and zealous preachers, and God's blessing on their labours, as in some other places of the land, so in the north parts, many became enlightened by the Word of God, and had their ignorance and sins discovered unto them, and began, by His grace, to reform their lives and make conscience of their ways."

The Separatist movement was from the first distinctly spiritual in its character. As the eyes of its members were enlightened by the Holy Spirit, so they felt unable to remain within the mixed congregations of the various Anglican Churches. They desired to be free from what they described as "the base and beggarly ceremonies retained in the Church", and enforced by the "lordly and tyrannous power of the prelates (bishops)". They protested that it was contrary to the freedom of the gospel to burden men's consciences and make a profane mixture of persons and things in the worship of God. They maintained that the whole ecclesiastical system had no warrant in the Word of God. Bradford goes on, "So many, therefore, of these professors as saw the evil of these things in these parts, and whose hearts the Lord had touched with heavenly zeal for His truth, shook off this yoke of anti-Christian bondage, and as the Lord's free people joined themselves, by a covenant of the Lord, into a church estate, in the fellowship of the gospel."

Among the men whose ministry had been used in this connection was Richard Clyfton, Rector of Babworth, a village six or seven miles south of Scrooby. Bradford says he was "a grave and reverend preacher, who by his pains and diligence had done much good". He had come to Babworth in July 1586. Many years later as an old man in his New England home across the Atlantic, William Bradford recalled the name and memory of this good man, Richard Clyfton. To hear him in his youth Bradford had walked some nine miles from Austerfield on Sunday mornings. Richard Clyfton had been amongst those who went to Holland in exile, and Bradford says, "He was a grave and fatherly old man when he came first into Holland, having a great white beard; and pity is it that such a reverend old man should be forced to leave his country, and at those years to go into exile. But it was his lot, and he bore it patiently. Much good had he done in the country where he lived, and converted many to God by his faithful and painful ministry both in preaching and catechizing." Richard Clyfton was the spiritual father of many of those who formed the Scrooby Church, became their first pastor, and in 1608 went to exile with them to Amsterdam.

Another clergyman was Richard Bernard, Vicar of Worksop. He graduated at Cambridge in 1598 and first went to Epworth in Lincolnshire (later the home of John and Charles Wesley). He came to Worksop in 1601. He wrote a book entitled *The Isle of Man*, which is an allegory and very closely resembles Bunyan's book *The Holy War*. Richard Bernard was at one time so closely in sympathy with the Scrooby Church that they expected him to become a Separatist with them. He went so far as to set up a Congregational Church within the walls of his Parish Church, consisting of one hundred members who separated from the rest of the parish. But when the bishops began to take action against Separatists, he gave up his separation and remained within the Church of England, and from then onwards he entered into controversy with those who maintained a separate position. This action led John Robinson (the noted ministerial leader of the Pilgrim Fathers) to say to him, "A speech of your own uttered to myself (ever to be remembered with fear and trembling) cannot I forget, when after a conference between Mr. Helwisse and me, you uttered these words: 'Well, I will return home and preach as I have done, and I must say as Naaman did, The Lord be merciful to me in this thing.'"

Beside Richard Clyfton, who went forward even to exile, and Richard Bernard, who drew back, there were other Puritan ministers who came under the censure of bishops for showing signs of Separatism. These included Thomas Toller of Sheffield, Robert Gifford of Laughtonen-le-Northen, and Hugh Bromhead. The last of these three went into exile, leaving the Anglican Church, and giving as his reasons "that the profane ungodly multitude, without exception of any one person, are with them received into and retained in the bosom of the Church; these churches are ruled by and remain in subjection unto an anti-Christian and ungodly government, clean contrary to the institution of our Saviour Christ." Thus these men were led to see the scriptural pattern and principle of the separate individual congregation of baptized believers.

The view of Church government thus fostered by the ministry of many Puritan clergymen finally took shape in the formation of a Separatist congregation first of all in the town of Gainsborough in the year 1602. The town was remote from great cities, and provided access for quick flight to the Continent in days of persecution. The lords of the manor were the Hickman family, who in the days of persecution in the reign of Queen Mary, and in earlier times, had entertained such godly men as Bishop Hooper, John Foxe the Martyrologist, John Knox the Scottish Reformer and other godly ministers. They had also known exile in Antwerp for their beliefs. William Hickman, lord of the manor of Gainsborough from 1596 to 1625, had a godly background, and obviously nurtured rather than persecuted the little group of Separatist believers.

The first pastor of this Gainsborough Church was John Smyth, M.A., of Christ's College, Cambridge, where he graduated 1575-6. When driven from Gainsborough into exile, he practised as a doctor in Amsterdam. William Bradford speaks of him as an eminent man and a good preacher. He was pastor of the Gainsborough Church from 1602-1606. His hearers came to the gatherings from distances of up to ten to twelve miles. William Bradford and William Brewster walked from Austerfield and Scrooby with the rest of their group. This went on for three or four years, until, as Bradford tells us, "these people became two distinct bodies or Churches, and in regard of distance of place, did congregate severally; for they were of sundry towns and villages." Thus some time about 1605-6 those nearest Scrooby met at Scrooby, forming a Church in the old Manor House. Bradford says, "This second community met at William Brewster's house on the Lord's Day, and with great love he entertained them when they came, making provision for them, to his great charge."

There is no doubt that since his return from court, William Brewster "had done much good in the country where he lived in promoting and furthering religion, not only by his practice and example, and provoking and encouraging of others, but by procuring good preachers to the places thereabout". Here the venerable Richard Clyfton became pastor by free choice of the people. With him was another godly man named John Robinson. Robinson had originally preached at Norwich. He had studied at Cambridge University, and become a Fellow in 1598. Little is known about his birth and family, but it is clear that he studied at Cambridge from 1552 to 1598 in the days when the eminent Puritan, William Perkins, was there. On leaving the university, he became a minister somewhere in Norfolk, but from the very first seems to have been troubled by the vestments and ceremonies of the Church of England, and having begun to search the Scriptures, he says, "Had not the truth been in my heart, as a burning fire shut up in my bones (Jeremiah 29), I had never broken those bonds of flesh and blood, wherein I was so straitly tied, but had suffered the light of God to have been put out in mine own unthankful heart by other men's darkness." His scruples led to suspension as a clergyman, and suspension led to becoming pastor of a Separatist Church in the city of Norwich. There harassed by persecution, imprisonment and fines, he left his people at Norwich to seek refuge with the Scrooby Church. William Bradford, in referring to the Scrooby Church, says, "In this Church, beside Mr. Richard Clyfton, there was also that famous worthy man, Mr. John Robinson, who afterwards was their pastor for many years, until the Lord took him away by death."

Bradford goes on to speak of the persecution under which they met. Often they were compelled to leave Scrooby and meet elsewhere. Some were arrested and put in prison. Others were watched night and day. The records of the Church Court of the diocese of York contain many references to the persecution of the Separatists. December 1st, 1607 reads, "William Brewster of Scrooby, gentleman. Information is given that he is a Brownist, and disobedient in matters of religion." The Exchequer Record of the Archbishop of York, in the spring of 1608, reads, "Richard Jackson, William Brewster, and Robert Rochester of Scrooby in the county of Nottingham, Brownists or Separatists; for a fine of £20 a piece, imposed upon every one of them .... for causes ecclesiastical within the province of York, for not appearing upon lawful summons at the collegiate Church of Southwell, 22nd day of April."

Thus they were remorselessly hunted, and seeing little hope of living peaceably in their own country, by common consent resolved to cross the sea to Holland, where others had preceded them, and where they heard was freedom of religion for all men. Persecuted brethren in London and their brethren at Gainsborough had already settled peaceably in Amsterdam, and their numbers were continually being increased by new arrivals from most of the counties of England. In the autumn of 1607 the little Church at Scrooby therefore resolved to try and get to Holland as best they could. The obstacles were great, as they abandoned their homes, their land, their livings, and set out for a country whose language they would have to learn. Many of them were farmers, but some were scholars of Cambridge University. And as they tried to leave, they broke an ancient Act of Parliament of Richard II, which made emigration illegal without permission from the Government. This meant they had to leave their native land by stealth at night, paying captains of ships exorbitant rates of passage. Many attempts were made to get away in separate parties. They were often betrayed, captured and had their goods confiscated. Bradford refers to two memorable occasions as they attempted to get away across the open sand dunes of the coast of Norfolk.

CHAPTER 2

Exiles for Conscience Sake

Escape to Holland 1607-1608

The first of the two attempts to escape took place in the autumn of 1607, probably in the month of September. On the 30th September William Brewster was no longer Master of the Posts at Scrooby. The Government records show that he was succeeded by Francis Hall on the 1st October, 1607. Also in the Church Court at York there is a record dated 15th September, 1607, which states that a man called William Blanchard was given the right to arrest William Brewster of Scrooby for Brownism, but had reported that he was unable to find him. Besides Brewster his neighbour Thomas Helwisse was one of the foremost organisers of the escape. Of him John Robinson said, "He, above all, furthered this passage into strange countries; if any brought oars, he brought sails." On June 26th Helwisse's wife, Joan, was under arrest in York Castle, and was brought before an Ecclesiastical Court in York on that day.

These men were therefore resolved to look for peace in a country across the sea. To do this, they decided to move as a body, and not in small groups, and to make for Boston on the Lincolnshire coast as their point of departure. They came to an agreement with the captain of a ship to meet them at a convenient place on a certain day, but the captain, while accepting the conditions, secretly betrayed them, and no sooner had they boarded his ship than they were arrested, put back into open boats, and taken back to Boston, where all their money and goods were taken from them. Crowds flocked to see them, and they were made an open spectacle to all. Here they were kept in the cells of the Guildhall, while the magistrates waited for an order to come from the Privy Council in London. The magistrates were not unfavourable to them, as Puritanism was strong in Boston. A quarter of a century later nine hundred Puritan colonists sailed for Massachusetts under the leadership of John Winthrop, and many leading citizens of Boston were among their number, including a Mayor, a Recorder, an Alderman and John Cotton, the Puritan preacher of Boston for twenty years, who became a leading Puritan in the New England Colonies. It was because so many of the people of Boston went to America between 1620 and 1630 that in September 1630 a settlement in the New England Colonies was named Boston.

Bradford tells us that "the magistrates used them courteously, and showed them what favour they could, though they could not deliver them until order came from the Council". What the Privy Council decided is not known, but after detaining them for a month, the magistrates sent the main body of prisoners back to their homes at Scrooby and elsewhere, and kept seven of their leaders still in prison. After a further period of detention, these were bound over to appear at the Assizes. One of these seven, Bradford tells us, was William Brewster, who "was chief of those that were taken at Boston, and suffered the greatest loss".

The failure of this attempt in the autumn did not stop them from making further efforts in the following spring. This time they decided to leave from the port of Hull. They made an agreement with a Dutch captain who came from Zealand, hoping to find him more reliable than their own countrymen. He arranged to take them on board at a lonely spot between Grimsby and Hull. The women went by way of Gainsborough and the River Trent, while the men made their way forty miles across open country. The two parties joined up at the agreed spot and waited in a small ship off the coast for the Dutch ship to arrive. The sea was rough and the women got the men to run the boat into a small creek where it might lie aground at low water. When the Dutch ship arrived the English boat was aground and could not be moved until high water at noon. The captain therefore decided to take some of the men on board. He had taken one boatload and was returning for the second, when he saw in the distance "a great company, both horse and foot, with bills, and guns and other weapons". He decided to abandon the rest of the Pilgrims, weigh anchor and set sail for Holland. Thus one party of the men found themselves the witnesses of the arrest of their wives, children and companions, while they themselves were helpless, and were conveyed away with only the clothes they stood up in. Their anguish of mind must have been great, added to which almost at once the ship ran into a tremendous storm which drove them towards Norway and prevented them reaching Holland for fourteen days. On the English coast some of the men stayed with the women and children, while others made good their escape.

The women and children were arrested, weeping and defenceless. They were brought before the magistrates, but none seemed eager to send them to prison for the crime of wanting to go with their husbands. On the other hand they now had no homes to which they could return as all had been sold before their attempt to escape. The captors were now faced with the problem of what to do with these defenceless women and children, and were only too glad to be rid of them. It is not clear what happened to them in the period between the failure of this second attempt and their eventual departure for Holland. Various people must have opened their homes to them and they rallied together under the leadership of John Robinson, William Brewster and the aged minister Richard Clyfton who "were of the last, and stayed to help the weakest".

William Bradford goes on to say in his account, "Notwithstanding all these storms of opposition they all got over at length, some at one time and some at another, some in one place and some in another," and that on a happier shore they "met together again according to their desires with no small rejoicing". The effect of their sufferings was to make them famous in England and many began to inquire what was the principle which moved them to undergo such sufferings. Also the effect was to stir up other weaker brethren who had at first hesitated. Bradford says, "Though some few shrank at these first conflicts and sharp beginnings (as it was no marvel), yet many more came on with fresh courage and greatly animated others." Their very enemies dragged them into fame, and "their godly carriage and Christian behaviour was such as left a deep impression on the minds of many".

Arrival in Holland 1608

On the Pilgrims' arrival in Holland the Dutch who had been at war with Spain were about to sign an armistice, which, when ratified in April 1609, was to last for twelve years. The exiles had arrived in Holland at the end of a long period of war, and were to leave it in 1620 for America, when Europe was to witness the beginning of the period of the "Thirty Years War." They first settled in the city of Amsterdam, which was well known for its Protestantism and liberty of speech. As far back as 1593 English Separatists had begun to come to Amsterdam in search of liberty. They had been members of the London congregation, and gradually as others were released from prison in London, they found their way out to their relatives in Amsterdam. When the exiles from Scrooby arrived, there were already two Separatist communities in Amsterdam, one from London under its pastor, Francis Johnson, and the other from Gainsborough under the care of John Smyth.

Francis Johnson was a graduate and Fellow of Christ's College, Cambridge. He had been minister of the church of the English merchants at Middleburgh in Zealand, and while there in 1591, as an Anglican clergyman, he had intercepted some of the books of the Separatists, which were being secretly printed at Dort. He communicated with the English ambassador, and received permission to have all the books burnt. A couple he saved for a friend and himself, and after reading his copy, was remarkably led to join the Separatists. Returning to London to talk with some of them in the prisons, he was eventually arrested and put in prison himself. He stayed in prison until March 1597, and the Privy Council gave him and several others permission to go out to Canada to the island of Ranea to found a colony. The journey was a disaster; they were shipwrecked off the coast of Newfoundland, captured by the French, and finally made their way back to Southampton as best they could. On reaching England, rather than face fresh imprisonment, they went over to Amsterdam with the rest of the London congregation.

It is possible that this story of an attempt to found a colony in North America became known to the Scrooby exiles. To this London church in exile came other exiles from almost all parts of England in search of freedom of worship. The Dutch marriage registers show at least one hundred and eighteen marriages between English exiles in the period 1598-1617, and state their original home place, from which it appears that they came from twenty-nine English counties, as well as from Wales. Northumberland, Yorkshire, Sussex, Kent, Cornwall, Devon, Norfolk, Suffolk are all represented. William Bradford, writing of these early days in Amsterdam as the Scrooby exiles came into contact with the earlier refugees, says, "Truly, there were many worthy men." About three hundred sat down to the Lord's Table.

The church from Gainsborough had gone out about 1606, and retained a separate existence under its pastor, John Smyth. This was possibly because Francis Johnson's church tended to be more Presbyterian in its government, and the later exiles from Gainsborough tended to believe in a more independent type of government. When the exiles arrived from Scrooby, they decided to worship separately under their pastor, Richard Clyfton, and their teacher, John Robinson. While Smyth held the view that authority in the church should be vested in the elders chosen by the congregation, Robinson believed that church authority should be vested in the Church of which the elders formed a part. In this respect, the Scrooby exiles contended against any powerful group of elders, and had clearer views regarding the authority of the church. They pointed out that such powerful eldership was not very different from the concept of bishops and priests.

After being in Amsterdam about a year, the Scrooby brethren, led by Robinson, decided to leave Amsterdam, and start church life afresh at Leyden, for they felt, as they said, "If we should let the true practice of the gospel go, posterity after us, being brought into bondage, might justly blame us that we did not stand for the rights of the people in that which we acknowledge to be their due." Bradford says, regarding this move to Leyden, "They well knew that it would be much to the prejudice of their outward estate both in the present and in the future, as indeed it proved to be." But their views of independent church government were strong, and believing this to be a vital point of difference, they decided to go away from their English brethren at Amsterdam.

Their application to settle in Leyden was accepted on the 12th February, 1609. It was a wealthy city of about one hundred thousand people, one which had stood firm against the Spaniards in a great siege, on account of which William of Orange had rewarded it by the granting of a charter for the foundation of the University of Leyden, 9th February, 1575. By the time the Scrooby exiles arrived, it was a famous university drawing students from all over Europe. One of the Professors of Theology, who died on the 19th October, 1609, was Arminius, the free-will theologian. The Scrooby exiles lived very much together as a community within a community. In 1611 they purchased a house in the name of Robinson, and it would appear that it was in part of this property that they worshipped while in Leyden.

Of their work Bradford says, "Being now pitched here, they fell to such trades and employments as they best could, valuing peace and their spiritual comfort above any other riches whatever." While most worked with their hands, William Brewster taught English to students in Leyden University. Later he set up a printing press, mainly for printing works connected with their Church. At Leyden, Robinson became the sole pastor, as Richard Clyfton had remained in Amsterdam partly because of his age and partly because he did not entirely agree with the Scrooby exiles regarding their views of eldership. So from 1609 to his death in 1625 John Robinson was the pastor of the brethren at Leyden. Of these days at Leyden Bradford says of the Church, "They continued many years in a comfortable condition enjoying much spiritual comfort together in the ways of God."

The Pilgrim Fathers at Leyden

On his arrival in Leyden in 1609, John Robinson had received a call from the English exiles to become pastor of their church, while William Brewster was appointed as his ruling elder. He considered it necessary to be ordained by the whole church. He says, "I was ordained publicly upon the solemn call of the church in which I serve, both in respect of the ordainers and the ordained." Ordination was for him a church act by the church concerned, and this act emphasised the Pilgrim Fathers' rejection of ordination by bishops, and of the use of patronage in the appointment of clergymen to livings in the Church of England. Robinson now frequently attended lectures at the University of Leyden, and eventually became one of its members. He was thirty-two at the time and soon gained a reputation for his learning, and gracious influence, which he had over his congregation and those with whom he came in contact. Even his enemies in the Church of England called him "the most learned, polished and modest spirit that ever separated from the Church of England".

Governor Bradford in his account *A History of Plymouth Plantation*, says of Robinson, "As he was a man learned, and of solid judgment, and of a quick, sharp wit, so was he also of a tender conscience, and very sincere in all his ways, a hater of hypocrisy and dissimulation, and would be very plain with his best friends. He was very courteous, affable and sociable in his conversation, and towards his own people especially. He was an acute and expert disputant, very quick and ready, and had much bickering with the Arminians, who stood more in fear of him than of any in the University. He was never satisfied with himself till he had searched any cause or argument he had to deal in thoroughly and to the bottom; and we have heard him sometimes say to his familiars that many times, both in writing and disputation, he knew he had sufficiently answered others, but many times, not himself; and was ever desirous of any light, and the more able, learned and holy the persons were, the more he desired to confer and reason with them. He was very profitable in his ministry, and comfortable to his people. He was much beloved of them, and as loving was he unto them, and entirely sought their good for soul and body. In a word, he was much esteemed and reverenced of all that knew him, and that were acquainted with his abilities, both of friends and strangers."

This description by Bradford, who is never given to flattery or exaggeration, presents us with a picture of a godly, gracious pastor, who drew his people together around his life and conversation, and under the truths which he preached. Whilst he was a man of peace, he was also a man of much wisdom. It was he who had seen the necessity that he and his people should leave Amsterdam, in order to stand firm for independent church government, rather than stay and enter into strife with those who remained. Yet in defence of the truth he was a warrior, who knew how to wield "the sword of the Spirit, which is the word of God". Bradford says, "Besides his singular abilities in divine things, he was able also to give direction in civil affairs, and to foresee danger and inconveniences; by which means, he was very helpful to their outward estates; and so was every way as a common father unto them. And none did more offend him than those that were close and cleaving to themselves, and retired from the common good; as also such as would be stiff and rigid in matters of outward order, and inveigh against the evils of others, and yet be remiss in themselves, and not so careful to express a good conversation. They in like manner had ever a reverent regard unto him, and had him in precious estimation, as his word and wisdom did deserve."

The Pilgrim church in Leyden grew under the pastoral care of John Robinson and William Brewster, and many exiles from various parts of England came out to join them, so that the congregation increased, and reached between two and three hundred people. Various matters of church order had to be dealt with, but for the most part, they were for the church years of "much sweet and delightful society, and spiritual comfort together in the ways of God". He himself had strong views about the part which the right call of a pastor to a congregation played in the peace and good order of a church. Robinson himself says, "It much furthers the love of the people to the person of their minister, and so, consequently, their obedience unto his doctrine and government, when he is such an one as they, in duty unto God, and love of their own salvation, have choice; as, on the contrary, it leaves them without excuse, if they either perfidiously forsake, or unprofitably use such a man's holy service and ministration."

Bradford gives an ideal picture of the love of the people for their pastor, and vice versa. He says, "It was hard to judge whether he delighted more in having such a people, or they in having such a pastor." They valued his ministry, and felt their loss deeply when he died in 1625. Of the period of his ministry at Leyden Bradford comments, "I know not but it may be spoken to the honour of God, and without prejudice to any, that such was the true piety, the humble zeal and fervent love of this people towards God and His ways, and the single-heartedness and sincere affection one towards another, that they came as near the primitive pattern of the first churches, as any other church of these later times have done according to their rank and quality." He writes, "They lived together in love and peace all their days without any considerable difference, or any disturbance that grew thereby, but such as was easily healed in love; and so they continued until they, with mutual consent, moved into New England (U.S.A.) . . . Many worthy and able men there were among them who lived and died in obscurity in respect of the world, as private Christians, yet were they precious in the eyes of the Lord, and also in the eyes of such as knew them."

When some of the clergy of the Church of England published books and pamphlets attacking the exiles for their separation from the Established Church, John Robinson was able to refute them by referring to his own congregation at Leyden: "I tell you that if ever I saw the beauty of Zion, and the glory of the Lord filling His tabernacle, it hath been in the manifestation of the divers graces of God in the church, in that heavenly harmony and comely order wherein, by the grace of God, we are set, and walk, wherein if your eyes had but seen the brethren's sober and modest carriage one towards another, their humble and willing submission unto their guides in the Lord, their tender compassion towards the weak, their fervent zeal against scandalous offenders, and their longsuffering towards all, you would, I am persuaded, change your mind, and be compelled, like Balaam, to take up your parable, and bless where you proposed to curse."

Others, beside their pastor, witnessed to the blessing of the Lord which rested among them in the days of their exile in Leyden. Edward Winslow, an able and educated young English gentleman, from Droitwich, came to Leyden in 1617, and was so drawn to the exiles that he joined them, and eventually sailed with them to New England, where he became a leader among the Pilgrim Fathers. Writing a quarter of a century later, he says, "I persuade myself never upon earth lived more lovingly together, and parted more sweetly than we, the Church at Leyden, did; parting not rashly in distracted humour, but upon joint and serious deliberation, often seeking the mind of God by fasting and prayer, whose gracious presence was not only found with us, but His blessing upon us from that time until now." Other gracious men who joined them in Holland included Thomas Brewer, a wealthy Puritan from Kent, John Carver, an early deacon of the Church, and leader of the first group of emigrants; also Robert Cushman, another of the early leaders.

David Fountain in his book *The Mayflower Pilgrims and their Pastor* says, "There was in Robinson a love of peace combined with a discernment and ardent love of the truth. While he was more ready to settle contentions by the meekness and gentleness of heavenly wisdom, rather than by carnal partiality, whenever he believed the truth to be at stake he did his duty. Arguments about matters that were not vital he left alone, but anything that damaged the church of God was, to him, of great concern, and, if need be, controversy." Thus we find Robinson defending the truth at Leyden against the free-will doctrine of Arminius. In this controversy it becomes quite clear that he held the doctrines of the Church of England regarding predestination as stated in the Thirty-nine Articles. This was not altogether strange since he greatly valued the sound ministry at Cambridge of the godly Puritan, William Perkins.

When the whole matter rose to such heights of controversy in the University of Leyden in 1612, Robinson was invited to support the free grace party in the University led by Polyander against the free-will leader, Episcopius. Bradford says, "When the time came, the Lord did so help him to defend the truth and foil his adversary, as he put him to an apparent nonplus in this great and public audience. And the like he did two or three times upon suchlike occasions; the which, as it has caused many to praise God that the truth had so famous a victory, so it procured him much honour and respect from those learned men, and others which loved the truth." This extract refers to various public debates in the city of Leyden in which Polyander and Robinson and others contended from the Scriptures against Episcopius on the question, "Were men saved through the grace of God alone, or were they (as Arminius said) capable of cooperating with God in their own salvation?"

While at Leyden, Robinson published several works. One of the earliest was *The Justification of Separation from the Church of England*, printed in

1610. It would appear that this book was widely read in England, and was the means in the following years of bringing many to his Church at Leyden. He continued writing and preaching until his death in 1625 at the age of fifty. He never went to the New England Colonies, though he often wrote to the Pilgrims, warning, exhorting and encouraging them. He lies buried in Pieterskerk in Leyden, where a memorial was erected to him by the General Society of Mayflower Descendants in the U.S.A. in 1928.

CHAPTER 3

In Search of Freedom

The Pilgrim Fathers leave Holland

There are many reasons why the Pilgrim Fathers decided to leave Holland. Their lives were hard as they laboured with their hands to provide themselves a living in a foreign country. They were also concerned about the condition of their children. Some had joined the Dutch army, others had become sailors in the Dutch merchant ships, and some had entered godless lives, greatly to the sadness of their parents. The Pilgrims found themselves unable to give their children much education, and they were also grieved by the desecration of the Lord's Day, which was prevalent in Holland at this time. Further, they were Englishmen, heart and soul, and they longed to have a country of their own and have their religious freedom there. Finally, Bradford says, "An inward zeal they had of laying some good foundation or at least to make some way thereunto, for the propagating and advancing of the kingdom of Christ in those remote parts of the world; yea, though they should even be as a stepping stone unto others for the performing of so great a work."

They were also not beyond the reach and harassment of the English King, James I. Correspondence of the English ambassador at The Hague, Sir Dudley Carleton, shows that the King used him to obtain the arrest of some of the Pilgrims, for printing books which were against the Church of England. He was particularly anxious to have William Brewster arrested, for his part in printing such books; in fact a man was arrested but it transpired that his name was Brewer, who was also involved in printing these books in Holland. After some very complicated legal moves Brewer eventually agreed to go to England, under safe conduct from the government of James I, and was examined there, before he returned to Holland. When the *Speedwell* sailed in 1620 Brewer appears to have stayed with Robinson in Holland, but after the death of Robinson he returned to England about 1626 and lived in Kent, but it was not very long before he was arrested and spent the next fourteen years in prison. He was released in 1640 by the Long Parliament, just at the beginning of the Civil Wars.

There was therefore every reason in the minds of the Pilgrims why they should found a Puritan colony and try and obtain liberty of worship abroad, in their own country. Elizabeth I had considered how she might rid herself of some of the Puritans in England,

and it had been suggested to her that she send them to the province of Ulster in Northern Ireland. But she had never acted on this advice and James I ruled it out also as a solution to the Puritan problem in his realm. John Robinson had thought of taking his people to the West Indies, but they faced tropical lands, dangerous diseases and the Spanish colonists; and it had not been long before this that the Protestant settlers in Florida had been massacred by the French.

As early as 1606 some London merchants had received from King James I a patent allowing them to establish the Virginia Company. It consisted of two branches, commonly known as the London and Plymouth Companies. The former had its head-quarters in London, and was known as the Virginia Company, with jurisdiction from 34° to 38° northern latitude. The latter, the Northern Company, had its seat of management in Plymouth, with jurisdiction from 41° to 45° northern latitude. The intervening territory was to go to whichever of the two Companies should first plant a self-supporting colony there.

The Virginia Colony had a very chequered existence and was mainly peopled by those who went out to escape a hard life at home. Under the patent granted to the Virginia Company, all the colonists had to conform to the Church of England. This obviously would not suit the Pilgrims for they might as well return to England as go out to such a colony. Yet they thought that it might be possible to come to some arrangement with the King, whereby they might go to Virginia and still enjoy their religious freedom. With this in mind two of the Pilgrims, Robert Cushman and John Carver, were sent over to England to negotiate with the Virginia Company. The Company was anxious to obtain some emigrants of character and reliability and were willing to try to obtain from the King a concession for liberty of religion.

To make this possible the brethren from Leyden submitted, through the Virginia Company to the King, a series of seven *Articles*, which the Church at Leyden sent to England to be put before the Virginia Company Council and the King. In these Articles they owned their allegiance to the Thirty-nine Articles of the Church of England, and to His Majesty King James I as sovereign ruler over his own kingdom to whom all obedience was due, if the things commanded by him were not against the Word of God. They agreed that His Majesty could appoint bishops and acknowledged the authority of bishops in the land so far forth as is indeed derived from His Majesty, but they added that they did not believe in any Synod, Convocation or Assembly of ecclesiastical officers having any power at all, but as the same is by the magistrate given to them.

These *Articles* were signed by John Robinson as the pastor and William Brewster as the elder. They were received by the Virginia Council on 12th November, 1617, while Cushman and Carver went back to Leyden and reported to the church the results of their interview with the Virginia Council. In trying to obtain freedom of worship in Virginia the Pilgrims of Leyden secured the powerful influence of Sir Edwin

Sands who prevailed upon Sir Robert Nanton to speak privately to the King, urging him to grant liberty of conscience under his gracious protection in America. The King appeared to be about to give way in this matter but decided to consult the Archbishop of Canterbury and the Bishop of London, and here he met with strong opposition, for the bishops did all they could to stop freedom for the "Brownists", as they called them, in Virginia. While the leading men on the Virginia Council found it impossible to obtain under the King's seal the right of religious freedom, it nonetheless appeared fairly clear that if the Pilgrims went to Virginia, the King would probably leave them alone.

When the agents returned to the Church at Leyden the Pilgrims gathered together to discuss the matter. Some felt that a venture on such sandy foundations was too dangerous, but their leaders took a more hopeful view of the situation. They took the view that the King would allow them freedom, though he had reasons of his own for not signing any document to that effect; and even if he had, he could always revoke it at any time, so that they would still have no real guarantee of religious liberty. Their leaders felt that there was a reasonable opportunity open to them and that for the rest they must trust in the Lord's guiding and protecting hand.

The Church at Leyden then arranged a special day of humiliation, thanksgiving and prayer to seek the Lord's direction. John Robinson preached on the occasion; his text was I Samuel 23. 3, 4, "David's men said unto him, 'Behold we be afraid here in Judah. How much more then if we come to Colah against the armies of the Philistines?' Then David inquired of the LORD yet again. And the LORD answered him and said, 'Arise, go down to Colah: for I will deliver the Philistines into thine hand.'" After the sermon a prayer meeting was held. It was an hour of great concern. It was finally decided that only part of the Church should go to America and the rest should remain at Leyden. The youngest and strongest should lead the way and only those should go who freely volunteered to do so. If a majority of the Church should wish to leave, the pastor should go with them; if a minority, then their elder William Brewster should lead the Pilgrims. It was further agreed that if the enterprise should fail, then those remaining behind should welcome back the returning Pilgrims to Leyden. But if it were successful then those who went first should afterwards help over the poor and older members of the Church.

There then occurred a serious dispute within the Virginia Company as a result of which nothing further was done about the Leyden expedition. In the meantime the Pilgrims at Leyden had been in contact with Dutch traders in Manhattan, the trading post afterwards known as New York. They had proposed to Robinson that they would transport his entire congregation to this trading post, providing cattle and furnishing protection, and leave them to govern themselves. An application was made on 12th February, 1620 to the Stadtholder in Holland, asking for the protection of the Dutch Government, which was referred to the Dutch States General. On 11th April it was rejected, but it appears that Robinson had already abandoned negotiations with the Dutch merchants. A letter from him to Carver on 14th June, 1620 made this clear.

A man named Thomas Weston had now come over from England offering the English Pilgrims financial help from himself and seventy other English merchants, who were prepared to back the emigration scheme of the Church at Leyden as a business enterprise, on the understanding that at the end of seven years there should be a division between the shareholders and the inhabitants of all the colony's possessions and earnings. The scheme was to be financed by ten pound shares. On this understanding articles were signed by both parties and Carver and Cushman were sent over to England to receive the money subscribed by the Merchant Adventurers (as Weston's associates came to be called), and make provision for the ships and necessary equipment for the voyage.

The brethren at Leyden prepared quickly to sell their property and get ready to emigrate. They put their money into a common stock. The original patent granted by James I in 1606 to the London Merchants for the Virginia Company had consisted of the two branches, the London and Plymouth groups, as already explained. Now in 1620 the Merchant Adventurers began thinking about New England, and the government charter of the Plymouth Company with jurisdiction from 41°. to 45° northern latitude was revived. The Merchant Adventurers thought that the fisheries off the New England Coast might be better than the coast nearer Virginia. So on 12th February, 1620 the "Wincob" patent was superseded by a patent granted to John Pierce, one of the Merchant Adventurers, which conferred powers of self-government and the right to a tract of land to be selected near the mouth of the Hudson River by the planters themselves.

In addition to the emigrants from Leyden the expedition was to be joined by a contingent from England, and one of their number, Christopher Martin, an Essex man, joined with Carver and Cushman in carrying out the arrangements for the expedition. When all was ready for the commencement of the expedition a pilot was sent over to Holland to bring the emigrants to England. He brought a letter announcing that the *Mayflower*, a vessel of 180 tons, was to start from London to Southampton, bringing the English party to meet them at Southampton. Also a 60 ton pinnace, the *Speedwell*, had been bought by the Merchant Adventurers, and was being fitted out in Holland to bring the Leyden people to Southampton and afterwards accompany the *Mayflower* across the Atlantic, remaining with the colonists for a year. And thus Bradford says, "After much travail and many debates their children may see with what difficulties their fathers wrestled in going through these great things in their first beginnings and how God brought them along, notwithstanding all their weaknesses and infirmities."

Now the brethren in the Church at Leyden prepared to separate. First they joined in a day of solemn humiliation. John Robinson preached the last sermon the Pilgrims were ever to hear from his lips; the text was Ezra 8. 21, "Then I proclaimed a fast there at the river Ahava, that we might afflict ourselves before our God, to seek of him a right way for us, and for our little ones, and for our substance." Bradford says he spent a good part of the day very profitably and suitable to the present occasion.

Finally they prepared to leave Leyden and travel along the canal to Delfshaven which took about six to eight hours. Thus they left the city which had been their resting place for twelve years. "They knew they were pilgrims and looked not much on earthly things, but lifted up their eyes to heaven their dearest country and quieted their spirits" (Edward Winslow). It was a July day that they left Leyden and finally arrived at Delfshaven to find the *Speedwell* at anchor at the quay. It was a very sad parting. Bradford describes it saying, "Loath to depart, their reverend pastor fell down on his knees and they all with him while he with watery cheeks commended them with most fervent prayers to the Lord and His blessing."

It was about 22nd July, 1620 as they hoisted sail, with a volley of shot from their muskets, followed by the booming sound of shots from three of the ship's cannon. They had a good run to Southampton where the *Mayflower* was riding at anchor having preceded them from London carrying the English portion of the emigrants. In the ship, anchored at the West Quay at

Southampton, were labourers employed by the merchants and also some godly Englishmen who sympathised with the Pilgrims' stand for religious freedom.

While at Southampton the Pilgrims received two letters from Robinson, one to Carver, the other to the whole body. In the letter addressed to them all, Robinson exhorted them to be on their watch, especially regarding their conduct on what was to be a very trying and tedious voyage and to seek the Lord's help not to give offence to others especially the worldly among them, so that they would not bring reproach on the truth. He ended with the words, "Fare you well in Him in whom you trust and in whom I rest." This letter was read aloud to them all and then after final arrangements in which ninety of the company were assigned to the *Mayflower* and thirty to the *Speedwell*, on 5th August, 1620 the two vessels set sail from Southampton West Quay and were soon down Southampton Water out past the cliffs of the Isle of Wight and out into the English Channel.

The Pilgrim Fathers leave Southampton

The progress of the Pilgrim Fathers down the Channel was slow. After a few days the captain of the *Speedwell* reported that his ship had sprung a dangerous leak and they had to put into Dartmouth. After repairs they put to sea again but there was further trouble. Some three hundred miles beyond Land's End the ship developed another leak and appeared to be unseaworthy, so they returned to

Plymouth. Once there, it was finally determined to send the *Speedwell* back to London to the Merchant Adventurers with eighteen of the passengers who had grown faint-hearted. The remaining twelve passengers were added to the already overcrowded *Mayflower*. Bradford, commenting in his *Journal* on this part of the journey says, "Like Gideon's army this small army was divided, as if the Lord by this work of His providence thought these few too many for the great work He had to do."

On 6th September they turned the prow of their ship once more to the west. The wind was with them and continued so for many days until they were half-way over the Atlantic when the equinoctial gales came sweeping down upon them with tremendous force, shaking the *Mayflower* from stem to stern, and so twisting one of her main beams out of its place that even the sailors began to be alarmed. One of the passengers who had brought a powerful screw with him was able, with the help of the sailors, to put the beam back into position. Once more they committed themselves to God determined to go forward. Storm succeeded storm, with fierce winds so strong that for days together not a sail could be spread; the boat was driven before the gale under bare poles. Crowded below for safety, their bedding and clothing drenched with water as huge waves chased each other day and night over the vessel, these poor Pilgrims in search of liberty must have longed earnestly for "their desired haven". One of their number, when washed overboard, managed to lay hold of a coil of rope by which he was pulled back on board again. Through God's mercy, though the ship was badly overcrowded, only one passenger, a servant, Samuel Fuller, died. Three days after his burial on 9th November, nine weeks after leaving Plymouth Harbour, to the great joy of all the Pilgrims, land was sighted.

Now began a long search for a suitable spot in which to settle. They were off Cape Cod, well south of the Hudson river, where they originally intended to land. Here firstly they signed a compact, the famous *Mayflower Compact*. Every man was to have an equal voice in making the laws. All the heads of the families, forty-one in number, set their names to it, and John Carver was chosen to be their first governor.

The *Compact* was subscribed *Cape Cod, 11th November, 1620*. It read: "In the name of God, Amen. We, whose names are under-written, the loyal subjects of our dread sovereign Lord, King James, by the grace of God, of Great Britain, France and Ireland, King, Defender of the faith, etc., having undertaken, for the glory of God and advancement of the Christian faith, and honour of our King and country, a voyage to plant the first colony in the northern parts of Virginia, do by these present solemnly and mutually in the presence of God, and of one another, covenant and combine ourselves together into a civil body politic, for our better ordering and preservation, and furtherance of the ends aforesaid, and by virtue hereof to enact, constitute and frame such just and equal laws, ordinances, acts, constitutions and offices as from time to time shall be thought most meet and convenient for the general good of the Colony, unto which we promise all due submission and obedience." The *Compact* was signed by about forty men, the first six names being John Carver, William Bradford, Edward Winslow, William Brewster, Isaac Allerton, and Miles Standish.

Having rounded Cape Cod they found shelter in a quiet harbour, and here the *Mayflower* lay at anchor while the Pilgrims searched the bay to find a suitable place to site their first settlement. On 15th November a group went on foot, and though they met Indians the Indians fled at their approach, and after some time they returned to the ship. Their small boat being ready on 27th November, a second expedition set out; it encountered heavy seas and cold weather as they searched the bay. A third expedition set out on 6th December, and sailed up the coast about twenty miles. While on land they were attacked by Indians, and a shower of arrows fell on them as they breakfasted, but mercifully no one was injured and a musket shot scattered the Indians. They met with snow storms and rough seas in the Bay until they came to a small island, which they named Clarks Island after the man that first stepped ashore on it, and from here they first entered Plymouth Harbour.

The next day was Saturday and they spent it repairing their little boat. On the Sabbath they rested. On 11th December they sounded the harbour and found it suitable for shipping; also walking around the area they found several cornfields and running brooks. They felt the place very suitable for their first settlement. Here, setting foot on Plymouth Rock they had at last reached their long-sought-for resting place. The Pilgrims in the *Mayflower* lying at anchor twenty-five miles away anxiously awaited the return of their little ship. Sad to say, when they returned, William Bradford learned to his sorrow that his wife, Dorothy May of Wisbech, Cambridgeshire, whom he had married in Amsterdam seven years before, had fallen overboard and was drowned. Thus their path, chequered at every step, was a matter for the deep trial of their faith. Within a day or two the *Mayflower* herself was in Plymouth Bay, beaten by storms, but her work was accomplished, and the Pilgrims were safely landed in their New England home ready to possess their freedom.

CHAPTER 4

A New Home - Plymouth Colony

Arrival in America

This freedom was to be purchased under very severe conditions. When they had left Holland it had been their hope that they would reach America before the winter had set in. But due to the many delays, especially the return of the *Speedwell* and the Atlantic storms they had arrived on the North American coast in the very depth of the winter. On landing, all the men in the company toured the region around Plymouth, previously picked by the exploring party, and eventually, after a vote had been taken, it was decided to settle in the area suggested. That same afternoon twenty of the men put up barricades and decided to spend the night on shore, the others returning to the ship. That night a tremendous storm burst over the coastal area, and the *Mayflower* had to use all her three anchors to stand the strain of the storm, nor could the people on board get any food to the shore party until late the next day. Then all the men went ashore to start building a common house about twenty feet square for communal use until they could all build their own houses. Each night the majority returned to the ship while twenty men stayed on shore to guard their building. On Sunday, 24th December, they were alarmed by a company of Indians letting out war cries, and though they never actually caught sight of them, it put them on their guard. Monday, 25th, was Christmas Day, but as their journal reported, "no man rested all that day". Within four days their timber building was up and thatched. They then erected a platform on the hill on which they placed one of the ship's cannons, in case the Indians tried to attack them.

The whole company was now divided into nineteen families, single men being assigned to families. It was arranged that each family should build their own house. These houses were to be built so as to form a single street, parallel with the stream which they called *The Townbrook*. Since 1823 the street has been called Leyden Street and still leads up from Plymouth Rock and from the beach to the hill beyond. Within a very short space of time their buildings became essential to their survival, for as a result of the bitter winter, hard work, poor food, unhealthy crowding on the ship, illness began to spread rapidly among them. Now they lay sick and dying in their newly-built homes. In January and February 1621 they died at the rate of two or three a day, until at one time it seemed that the whole colony would be wiped out, for there were only six or seven able-bodied men left to carry out all the necessary work.

William Bradford, himself laid aside with illness, speaks with gratitude of William Brewster and Miles Standish as two who never succumbed and who were unceasing in their loving care for the sick. Bradford says: "What I have said of these, I may say of others who died in the general visitation, and others yet living, that, whilst they had health, yea, or any strength continuing, they were not wanting to any that had their need of them." The first house that was finished had to be used as a hospital, and by the end of February thirty-one of the Pilgrims had died. A little hill above the beach, now known as Coles Hill, was set apart for the burial place of the dead, the graves being levelled and grassed over, lest the Indians should discover how few and weak the settlers were becoming.

When spring came, of the hundred who had landed, only fifty survived. Their journal records, "Toward the end of March the sun began to be warm about noon and the birds sang in the woods." Now their long winter was over, but their dangers continued as wolves were heard howling in the woods at night and evidences were all about them of the continuing presence of Indians. Tools left in the woods often disappeared. Two Indians were seen on the hill on the other side of *The Townbrook*, but they quickly disappeared as some of the Pilgrims attempted to approach them. It soon became clear that in addition to their civil government, formed by their *Compact* on board the *Mayflower* they would have to establish a military organisation. This they did under the command of Miles Standish, and it was agreed to bring ashore the five cannon from the *Mayflower* and place them on a platform on Fort Hill, so that the guns commanded the approaches to the village on every side.

The first year of the colony

The first winter was filled with hardship and sadness, severe sickness, intense cold and dangers from surrounding Indian tribes. This situation did not change much during the next two or three years. Further sickness followed, food was scarce and great care had to be continually exercised in contact with the Indians. Also in the same period there were fresh arrivals of colonists sent out from England by the Merchant Adventurers, and the Pilgrims had to face insidious attempts by that trading company to infiltrate the colony with people who did not agree with their staunch independency, but wanted to introduce the system of bishops from which the Pilgrim Fathers had fled.

The fears of the colonists regarding the Indians were very real, though prior to the arrival of the Pilgrim Fathers at Plymouth Plantation the Indian tribes who had inhabited that area had been wiped out by the plague, and the colonists found the skeletons of thousands of Indians within a radius of twenty miles of their settlement. Unwittingly, and yet guided by the Lord's hand, they had settled in an area which was uninhabited, over which no tribe had any claim, and therefore they did not immediately come into conflict with the Indians as they might have done had they landed on any other territory along the coast. But they were bound to have contact with the Indian tribes about them, and again under the Lord's hand peaceful contact was established in a remarkable way.

Samoset - the Indian

One morning towards the end of March 1621 a solitary Indian walked down the main street of their settlement, came boldly towards them carrying his bow and arrows, and to their great surprise spoke to them in broken English. He told them his name was Samoset, that he was the chief of Monhegan, an island on the coast between the Kennebec and Penobscot rivers, where, from the men on the fishing boats, he had learnt English. He told them the Indian name for the place where they had settled was Patuxet or "Little Bay", and that four years ago the original Indians had all died of the plague. Their nearest neighbours to the west were Massasoit's people, a tribe of about sixty warriors, and to the east were the Nausets, who had attacked them while they had been exploring the bay. When Samoset left, he promised to return on the following day bringing with him some beaver skins. This he did in company with five tall Indians who, as a sign of peace, left their bows and arrows outside the settlement and brought back the tools which had been lost in the woods a month before. They offered to dance before them, and sell them their beaver skins.

As it was Sunday the Pilgrims declined the offer, but at the same time realised that the main object of their visit was to pave the way for the coming of the great Chief Massasoit himself.

Tisquantum - another Indian

The following Thursday Samoset reappeared, bringing with him another Indian who proved to be an invaluable friend to the settlers. This was Tisquantum, or Squanto, as he came to be called, the only man left of the Patuxet tribe, once living at Plymouth. The Lord's hand was again seen going out on behalf of the Pilgrim Fathers in that Tisquantum had lived for more than three years in London. He was one of twenty-four Indians who had been kidnapped by an English captain in 1614 and sold as slaves in Spain. Managing to escape he had made his way to England, where he had become a servant to various London merchants until in the early months of 1620 an English captain had brought him back to Plymouth Colony. Here he had found that all his tribe had died and he was the sole survivor. He had now come with Samoset to announce the approach of Massasoit the great chief of the confederate tribes of Pokanoket. The colonists realised that this first meeting would be of vital importance in establishing friendly relations with the Indian tribes.

Chief Massasoit

Within an hour the chief appeared with sixty of his warriors on the hill to the south of *The Townbrook*, and Tisquantum came into the colony to ask that a messenger be sent out to confer with their chief. It was a dangerous situation but Edward Winslow offered to go, and putting on his armour, crossed the stream and went up the hill alone to meet the Indians. Massasoit was very taken with his sword and armour and offered to buy them. Winslow greeted him in the name of King James I, King of England, and said that the governor of their colony, John Carver, wished to meet him to sign a peace treaty and discuss trade. Leaving Winslow as a hostage, Massasoit went down to the colony with twenty armed warriors. At the stream he was met by Captain Miles Standish and six musketeers, who escorted him to the town house, where, with all the carpets and cushions they could muster, Governor Carver, attended by a bodyguard of musketeers, received his distinguished guests with due ceremony, after which they ate and drank together.

A treaty with the Indians

The outcome of their meeting was a treaty by which each side agreed to refrain from attacking the other, and in the event of either being attacked, to assist each other. They also agreed that whenever they met in future, each side would come unarmed to such a meeting. In this way the Pilgrim Fathers entered into their first alliance and exercised the independence and sovereign power for which they had crossed the Atlantic. It is interesting to note that this treaty stood firm and was honourably observed for more than half a century. The treaty concluded, Samoset returned to his own tribe in the north while Tisquantum remained with the colonists as their valued friend, a memorable week indeed for the colonists. They had made friends with the people they expected to meet as foes and, no doubt, as they looked back the next Sabbath, it was with a sense of gratitude to the Lord, who had made even their enemies to be at peace with them. In April 1621 the *Mayflower* eventually raised anchor, hoisted sail and set her course for England, and now the Pilgrims were alone with the French five hundred miles away to the north in Nova Scotia and the English five hundred miles away in Virginia.

Planting the land

Much sorrow was theirs, for they worked under the hardships before them with the sad memory of those who had succumbed, men, women and children, buried on the little hill above the beach. But in that first spring they had little time to think about much else except the vital necessities of ploughing the land and sowing the corn. As strangers to the country they had little knowledge of what to plant or when. Tisquantum told them that Indian corn should be sown when the young leaves on the oak tree were as big as the ears of a mouse. He showed them how to fertilise the roots of their maize with a fish called ale-wives; he also told them when this type of fish would be most plentiful. Thus work went forward rapidly, some planting, some sowing, some felling timber and building, some hunting and fishing. After the dreadful sickness of the winter there were only twenty-one men and six strong lads capable of carrying out the necessary work. That spring twenty-one acres of land were sown with Indian corn, six acres with wheat, rye and barley, in addition to which they cultivated the gardens around their homes.

Death of John Carver

In the midst of these activities a great sorrow came upon them with the sudden death of their governor, John Carver. Returning from the cornfield one day in April 1621 and complaining of a pain in his head, he lay down, went unconscious and died two days later. Not long after his frail and delicate wife Katherine, worn out with the hardships, also passed away and was laid by his side in the same quiet resting place overlooking the sea. William Bradford was now elected governor, Isaac Allerton was appointed as his assistant and William Brewster continued as the principal preacher and minister.

Exploring the hinterland

As the summer of 1621 advanced Bradford desired to know more about the hinterland around their settlement, and also to maintain the contact already established with the Indian tribes. He accordingly sent out three or four expeditions. First Edward Winslow and Stephen Hopkins, with Tisquantum as guide and interpreter, set out to visit Massasoit, instructed by Bradford to carefully observe the country as they travelled through it. After walking for about twenty miles they reached his village, Sowams, now known as Warren on Narragansett Bay. Here they exchanged gifts and discussed the matter of corn which they had found buried when they first landed at Cape Cod the previous winter, asking to be allowed to pay the owners for what they had taken. Having stayed for a few days they returned by a different route, passing through country which must at one time have been thickly populated, but over which the plague had swept, leaving the unburied bones to mark the scene. They saw once-cultivated fields beside the streams and travelled through beautiful woods of oak, walnut, beech and chestnut trees, reaching home after an absence of about five days.

A second expedition went out in search of a son of one of the settlers who had lost his way in the woods around Plymouth Colony. Living on berries, the boy wandered for five days, over a distance of twenty miles until he was captured by the Nauset Indians. Hearing from Massasoit of the boy's whereabouts, ten well-armed men of the Pilgrims set out by boat to recover him, which they did at Buzzards Bay where the Indians handed him over. A third expedition went out in August 1621 led by Miles Standish with ten armed men. A rumour having reached Plymouth that Corbitant, the chief of the Pocassets, had captured Massasoit ,Tisquantum went on ahead to ascertain the truth of this and was captured by Corbitant who threatened to kill him. When Standish reached the village he found the chief had gone, leaving Tisquantum unharmed. Miles Standish returned to

Plymouth leaving a message for Corbitant that the Pilgrims would not tolerate any attack on Massasoit or their own settlement.

The effect of this prompt action brought six or seven Indian chiefs to sign peace treaties with the Pilgrims and acknowledge themselves as loyal subjects of King James I. The success of this expedition encouraged Bradford to send another to Massachusetts Bay to establish peace and trade with the Indians to the north, who they understood to be hostile to them. They succeeded in making friendship with the tribe of Shawmuts and also discovered the area now known as Boston Harbour which they realised would prove a suitable site for another settlement in days to come.

The end of the first year

They now entered the autumn of their first year in the colony and prepared for winter. Seven houses and four public buildings on the main street were now standing. One of the public buildings was used for worship and meetings, the others were used as store houses for food, and timbers ready to be sent back to the Merchant Adventurers in England. To celebrate the end of their first year the Pilgrims fixed a Thanksgiving Day. It was observed as a period of rest and a time to thank the Lord for the many mercies which they had received at His hand, not least peace with the Indian tribes around them. They also invited Massasoit with ninety of his tribesmen to be their guests for three days.

CHAPTER 5

Laying the Foundations

The Colony 1621 - 1624

Quite unexpectedly in November 1621 a ship, the *Fortune*, arrived at Plymouth Harbour with thirty-five new colonists, including William Brewster's eldest son, John Winslow, brother of Edward, and Robert Cushman. William Bradford says the plantation was glad of this addition to its strength, but could have wished that many of them had been of better condition, and all of them better furnished with provisions, but that could not be helped. The ship also brought a letter from the Merchant Adventurers complaining that the *Mayflower* had returned to England without any profitable cargo. The letter implied that the Pilgrims had not worked hard enough. It was addressed to their late governor, John Carver.

William Bradford, referring to the letter and its accusations wrote, "Touching John Carver he is departed this life and now is at rest in the Lord, and from all those troubles and encumbrances with which we are yet to strive. He needs not my apology, he who for the common good oppressed himself and shortened his days. If the Company have lost their profits these are not to be set over against the loss of the lives of honest and industrious men which cannot be valued at any price. It has pleased God to visit us with daily death, and with so great a general disease, that the living were scarce able to bury the dead, and the well, not in any measure to tend the sick; and now to be greatly blamed for not loading the ship at such a time doth indeed go near us and much discourage us." Bradford made sure that when the ship, the *Fortune*, returned she carried a good cargo of beaver fur, timber, and other commodities to the value of about five hundred pounds.

Indian hostility

Early in 1622 the colonists were disturbed by signs of hostility on the part of the Narragansett Indians. This was increased when news reached them from Virginia that on 22nd March the Indians had treacherously murdered practically the entire colony, killing about 347 men, women and children. This led the Pilgrim Fathers to construct a strong line of wooden fortifications around their colony with four towers and various gates which could be locked at night and guarded by sentries. Throughout the summer of 1622 the colonists were very short of food, especially bread, until the harvest was gathered in. To complicate matters another boat arrived from England with sixty more men who had come to start a new colony at Wessagusset, later known as Weymouth. They lodged with the Pilgrim Fathers for about six weeks till they went off to found their new colony.

Medical help for Massasoit

In the autumn of 1622 the Pilgrims' faithful Indian friend, Tisquantum, died of a fever. March 1623 brought them the news that their ally, Massasoit, was seriously ill at Sowams. They immediately sent Edward Winslow, who brought some simple medical treatment which resulted in the recovery of the Indian chief, who was ever after sincerely grateful to the Pilgrims for the kindness shown to him. Massasoit revealed to Winslow's interpreter, Hobomok, that the Massachusetts Indians were planning an attack. Their anger had been roused by the new settlement at Wessagusset on Boston Bay. These colonists had proved lazy and indisciplined; running short of food they had resorted to stealing from the Indians. They had contacted Governor Bradford to ask whether they should open war on the tribes around them, but Bradford could see that such action would destroy the peace conscientiously built up between the Pilgrims and the Indians; therefore he advised the new colonists to exist on groundnuts and shellfish as the Pilgrim Fathers had done at various times.

Miles Standish's attack on the Indians

The Indians had no grievance against the Pilgrim Fathers, but felt that if they attacked the settlement at Wessagusset they would inevitably have to attack the settlement at Plymouth. Bradford decided to act quickly. Miles Standish was sent with a body of armed men to Wessagusset to warn the new settlers there. They were quickly gathered together and then Miles Standish's men attacked and killed seven of the leading conspirators among the Indians, and after a battle on the following day routed the Indians. When Standish returned to Plymouth Colony it was decided to complete the fort on the hill, commenced about ten months before. From that time onwards the fort became the centre of the government and worship of the colonists, and around it they buried their dead.

Hunger and drought

Throughout 1623 life was no easier, and often the colonists did not know from where the next day's food was coming. At times they had to rely completely upon the sea for their food. At such times they divided themselves into groups of six or seven for the purpose of fishing, and as they had only one boat and one net, as soon as one company returned tired and worn out, another was ready to start. While the fishermen were away others went out at low tide on the sands to dig for shellfish. Others went into the woods in search of deer and various kinds of game.

Their difficulties were made worse by a period of seven weeks without rain in June and July of that year.

Their crop of maize began to wither, and famine appeared in sight. Winslow describes how he saw men staggering about through lack of food. William Brewster sat down to his table with a meagre wooden platter of boiled clams and a pot of water. Over this food he gave thanks to God that he and his were permitted to "suck of the abundance of the seas and of the treasures hid in the sand". As the drought continued they thought it good not only that every man should examine his own condition before God and his conscience, but that also publicly and solemnly they should gather together to humble themselves before the Lord in fasting and prayer. They continued in prayer for eight or nine hours without intermission, and have left it on grateful record that God was as ready to hear as they to ask.

Although when they met in the morning the sky was still cloudless, when they came out of the fort they could see clouds steadily gathering in the sky, and before many hours were passed, rain began to fall in softening showers on their dry fields. Day after day it continued to fall, until as Winslow says, "It was hard to say whether their withered corn or their drooping affections were most revived. Having these signs of God's favour and acceptation we thought it would be great ingratitude if secretly we should smother up the same, or content ourselves with private thanksgiving, and therefore another solemn day was set apart and appointed for that end, wherein we returned glory, honour and praise with all thankfulness to our good God who dealt so graciously with us."

New arrivals 1623

This thanksgiving had not been over long when a ship was seen entering the harbour at Plymouth. This proved to be the *Anne*, bringing about sixty new colonists and stores from the Merchant Adventurers in London. Ten days later she was followed by the *Little Jane*, a ship of forty-four tons carrying thirty-six more colonists. Some of these people were so obviously unfit for colonial life that the governor sent them back at once in the same boat at his own expense. Some had come out to follow an independent course of their own; the remainder were old friends and relations of the Pilgrims from the church at Leyden. Among these was George Morton and his household; Fear and Patience, the two daughters of Elder Brewster; the wife of Samuel Fuller; Mrs. Southworth, who later became the second wife of Governor Bradford, and Barbara, who subsequently married Miles Standish. These and the rest of the old friends from Leyden were warmly welcomed. But they were startled, having just left the cities of Europe behind them, to see the change wrought in those from whom they had parted at Delfshaven little more than two years before. Lack of food, constant exposure, hard work, had reduced them; their clothes were tattered and worn, their log cabins were unattractive, the best dish on their table was a piece of fish without bread or anything except a cup of water from the spring.

The "particulars" and the "generals"

For some time it was agreed that those who had come in the ship should live on the provisions they had brought with them, and that the produce of the land should belong to those who had tilled it. There was also a further complication: sixty of the emigrants who had come over were to be merged into the general colony, but there were about forty others who wished to form a separate colony within the colony, who described themselves as 'particulars' as distinct from the body of the colonists regarded as 'generals'. Behind this distinction was a subtle move instigated in London to eventually introduce into Plymouth Colony the rule of the Church of England, by gradually outnumbering the Pilgrim Fathers, with those who were not one with them in their stand for independent church government. With the newcomers added to those who came over in the *Mayflower*, plus the thirty-five brought by the *Fortune*, there had been two hundred and thirty-three pilgrims, or first-comers, or Forefathers, as the Americans have since known them. Out of these, at the end of 1623, there were about one hundred and eighty survivors.

Government of the colony

Government of the colony was mainly conducted through what was known as the Town Meetings, where everyone gathered and fresh laws were added as they were needed, but no Statute Book was considered necessary; an entry in the governor's notebook was deemed sufficient. Towards the end of 1623 a Colony

Record Book was started, the first entry dated the 17th December. This entry marks a step forward as it shows that the colonists had established "trial by jury"; all criminal matters, trespass and debt to be tried by the verdict of twelve honest men, to be empanelled in the form of a jury upon oath. On New Year's day, 1624, the colonists, for the third time, elected William Bradford as governor. He was far from happy at this, considering that the annual election was instituted to allow a change of governor each year. Notwithstanding his protest the townsmen re-elected him, at the same time creating a Council of five others who could advise him.

Letters from John Robinson

About the time of this election another ship, the *Charity*, arrived at Plymouth, bringing with it the last letters the colonists were to receive from their pastor, John Robinson, for whose coming they still continued to wait. One letter dated Leyden, 19th December, 1623, was addressed to Governor Bradford, in which he expressed his regret at hearing of the killing of the Indians by Miles Standish. He wrote, "How happy a thing it had been if you had converted some before you had killed any," and exhorted the Pilgrims to beware of the military spirit of Miles Standish. Robinson said that he loved Standish right well, was persuaded that God had given him to them in mercy and for much good if he used it aright. He feared that there might be wanting in him that tenderness of the life of man made after God's image, which is meek.

Robinson's second letter was addressed to William Brewster, and dealt mainly with the difficulties being raised by some of the Merchant Adventurers to stop himself and the rest of the brethren at Leyden from coming over to Plymouth colony. There were five or six men on the Board of the Merchant Adventurers who were warm friends of the Pilgrims, but there were another six who were opposed to the establishment of free worship in the colony. Robinson felt persuaded that they had purposes of their own to establish the Church of England form of worship and government in the colony. Feeling this hostility Robinson wrote to Brewster at the close of his letter, "Your God, and the God of all His, bring us together if it be His will and keep us in the meanwhile, and always to His glory, and make us serviceable to His Majesty and faithful to the end." Robinson was not far out in his surmise as to the purpose of the Adventurers.

Subtle influences from England

In 1623 another group of settlers had come out to the settlement at Wessagusset and brought with them an Anglican clergyman, William Morrell. This man spent a year at Plymouth, studying the Indians and various matters of natural history. Only when he had gone away did the Pilgrims realise that he possessed full powers from England, authorising him to compel the Pilgrim Fathers to conform to the Church of England, from which, at so great a cost, they had severed themselves. Then they began to realise that the 'particulars', who had come over in the *Anne*, formed the centre of this new movement. They had begun to send complaints back to London that there was religious controversy in the Colony, that the exercises on the Sabbath were neglected, the sacraments were disused, children were not catechised.

When the ship *Charity* arrived in 1624, bringing cattle and other supplies, she brought also a series of enquiries from the Merchant Adventurers about some of these complaints and also another Anglican clergyman, John Byford. At first this man, says Bradford, saluted them with reverence and humility, bowed and cringed before them, wept and shed many tears, blessing God, who had brought him to see their faces, and admiring the many things they had done. The Pilgrim Fathers felt he was altogether too effusive. Their misgivings were confirmed when they found him often engaged in conference with a man named Oldham and others of the 'particulars'. They came to realise he was sending defamatory letters back to London. Governor Bradford decided to intercept these letters, and found that the plan of Byford was to establish a Church of England. Oldham, leading the 'particulars', refused to do sentry duty at the fort under Standish, and eventually Byford and Oldham, with others, withdrew and set up public worship apart.

Governor Bradford decided to act. He summoned a court of the townsmen, and in the presence of all he charged Byford and Oldham with secretly plotting to destroy the government. They denied the charge, whereupon Governor Bradford produced Byford's letters, and read some of them, at which Byford was speechless. One of these letters contained advice that Robinson and the rest of the Church at Leyden should be kept out of the colony. Eventually the court decided to expel Oldham at once, and Byford was allowed to remain six months longer. If the colonists appeared intolerant they feared the object of these men was not so much religious equality as another Anglican domination from which they had fled.

CHAPTER 6

Home Rule

The Colony 1625 - 1627

The breach with Byford at Plymouth, New England, led to a breach with the Board of Merchant Adventurers at home. Edward Winslow, returning from a voyage to England in the early part of 1625, brought a letter from them saying they would only continue their connection with the Plymouth Plantation on certain conditions. One of the main reasons for their change of attitude was the ejection of Byford from the colony. The Merchant Adventurers called the Pilgrim Fathers, "Brownists", and said that as such they could not support them.

Breach with the Merchant Adventurers

The conditions of their co-operation for the future were as follows. Firstly, as they were partners in trade, they wished also to be partners in the colony, and desired the French or Presbyterian discipline to be adopted in substance and detail by the Pilgrim Fathers, so that the name of Brownists should be done away with. Secondly, they desired that pastor John Robinson, and the remaining members of the Church at Leyden should not be allowed to join the brethren at Plymouth, unless they should first agree to the system which the Merchant Adventurers spoke of as our church (that is, the Church of England). Thirdly they demanded that Robinson should agree to this by a written statement, signed by his own hand.

The Pilgrims replied to this letter saying they did conform to the discipline of the French and other reformed churches, as set out in the *Harmony of Confessions* of 1586, but they could not agree to tie themselves down to every particular detail of that discipline, saying that to do so would be to give away the liberty they had in Christ Jesus. Even Paul, they said, would have no man follow him except as he followed Christ. As regards Robinson and his friends at Leyden signing a recantation and agreeing to join the Pilgrim Fathers, Bradford makes no comment in his history. It was quite clear that there was no possibility of Robinson or any of the Pilgrim Fathers signing such a document.

Those of the Merchant Adventurers who still supported the Pilgrim Fathers wrote to them saying that a debt of one thousand four hundred pounds remained and this should be paid for by goods shipped as trade permitted. They expressed the hope that they would be enabled to pursue their way and that God, in

His providence, would work for them, as they felt persuaded the Pilgrim Fathers were the men who would make a plantation, where others would fail; and they added, "Go on, good friends, pluck up your spirits, and quit yourselves like men, in all your difficulties, so that in spite of all the displeasures and threats of men, the work to which you have put your hand may still go forward, a work which is so much for the glory of God, and the welfare of our countrymen."

In the summer of 1625 Miles Standish crossed the Atlantic to England, taking with him letters in reply to those they had received. James I had died at the end of March that year, and now his son Charles I was on the throne, and the full weight of Archbishop Laud was being felt, rigorously enforcing uniformity to the Church of England. In five months all that Standish could do was to obtain a loan of one hundred and fifty pounds at fifty per cent interest, to purchase goods for the colony. He returned in a fishing boat bound for the coast of Maine. Indian messengers reported his presence there, and the shallop was sent up the coast to bring him and his goods to Plymouth. He brought sad news: firstly the death of King James (though when this news reached them, he had been dead for more than a year); also Prince Maurice, the Dutch Ruler, had died; also their friend, Robert Cushman, who had been their principal leader in dealing with the Merchant Adventurers, had died at the early age of forty-five. But, saddest of all, Standish had to tell them that all hope of ever seeing John Robinson must be abandoned.

The death of John Robinson

There were also letters from Roger White, Robinson's brother-in-law, and Thomas Blossom, a leading member of the Leyden church, and a joint letter addressed to Bradford and Brewster telling them that their pastor had been taken ill on Saturday, February 22nd, and had entered into rest on 1st March, 1625. Roger White said in his letter, "If either prayers, tears, or means would have saved his life, he had not gone hence." Thomas Blossom spoke of "the loss of our beloved and honoured Pastor, whom the Lord, as it were, took away, even as fruit falleth before it is ripe, where neither length of days nor infirmity of body did seem to call for his end. The loss of his ministry", he said, "was very great indeed unto me, who ever counted myself happy in the enjoyment of it, notwithstanding all the crosses and losses otherwise I sustained."

The letter from the Church was signed by four of its members. They said, "It hath pleased the Lord to take to himself our dearly beloved pastor, yet for ourselves our mind is as formerly to come unto you, when the Lord affordeth means. And now, brethren, what shall we say to you further ? Our desire and prayer to God is, if such were His good will and pleasure, we might be reunited for the mutual comfort of both, which, when He sees fit, He will accomplish."

Winslow, speaking of the death of Robinson says, when God took him away from them and us by death the University of Leyden, and ministers of the city, followed him to his grave with all their accustomed solemnity, bewailing the great loss. Robinson was buried in Pieterskerk Leyden, near his own house. The church at Leyden continued to flourish for many years after and it is recorded that in 1658 it was united with the Reformed Church of Holland. In July, 1891, the National Council of Churches of the United States had a bronze memorial tablet fixed on an exterior wall of Pieterskerk, Leyden, to commemorate the burial of Robinson there.

About the time that the news reached William Brewster concerning the death of Robinson, his own wife passed away at the age of fifty-six. Trouble still gathered around the Puritans, yet, as Bradford says of these sad days, the Lord, whose work they had in hand so helped them that now, when they were at their lowest they began to rise again; being stripped in a manner of all human helps and hopes. The Lord brought things about otherwise in His divine providence as that they were not only helped and sustained, but their proceedings were both honoured and imitated by others as by the sequel the more appeared. The agriculture of the colony began to prosper, more maize was grown than they needed, and they found they could get a ready sale for the surplus at six shillings a bushel.

More prosperity - trade increases

They now began to desire more trade with their neighbours, and hearing that a trading post at Monhegan was about to be broken up and the stock offered for sale, Governor Bradford and Edward Winslow went over and acquired about half the goods for four hundred pounds. About the same time a French ship with a cargo of rugs and other commodities was wrecked at Sagadahoe. Goods from this wreck were acquired by the colonists through some Bristol merchants. They paid for it in beaver fur, and other goods for barter. They were now better furnished for trade, and were able to meet their various engagements, getting clothing for their people and having things in stock. One serious difficulty lay in the way of extending their trade. They had only one small open boat, and it was dangerous to use this for long voyages, especially during the winter. The ship's carpenter having died, the house carpenter took the matter in hand, and extended the boat some five or six feet, built it up, made a deck, and fitted sails. This did them good service for seven years and enabled them to build up their trade.

The "Undertakers" and the "Purchasers"

It was then that they decided to break off their connection with the Merchant Adventurers completely. Isaac Allerton was sent to England in 1626 and came to an agreement with a Company in London whereby the Merchant Adventurers gave up all claim to stock, shares, land, etc. at Plymouth colony, the colonists agreeing to pay one thousand eight hundred pounds at the place appointed for the receipt of money on the west side of the Royal Exchange in London; this money to be paid in sums of two hundred pounds yearly on the Feast of St. Michael; the first payment to be made in 1628, and the whole to be completed over nine years. This agreement was signed by Bradford, Brewster, Standish, Allerton, Winslow, on behalf of the colonists, they being liable for the money. Accepting the responsibility of this money, those who signed obtained the consent of the rest of the colonists to be allowed sole responsibility for all trade of the colony with the outside world. Each of the Pilgrim Fathers would pay to this group of senior men three bushels of corn, or six pounds of tobacco as might be preferred, and it was hoped that the whole could be paid off within six years. When the debt was paid the trade of the colony would once more return to the individual Pilgrim Fathers as they saw fit to undertake it themselves.

Bradford, Brewster, Standish, and the others who undertook this responsibility were afterwards known as the "Undertakers". In this way the property passed from the Merchant Adventurers to the colonists and for six years from the colonists to the "Undertakers". A deed to this effect was taken over to England by Allerton in the following year. Thus, while the responsibility for the payment of the outstanding debt rested with Bradford, Brewster, Standish, Allerton, Winslow, Howland, Alden and Prince, it was divided among the colonists by their yearly payment of corn and tobacco, and it was agreed that, if profits were not sufficient to meet the yearly payments in London, the deficiency should be made up in equal proportions by the settlers who were described as "Purchasers" in the deed.

In return for this liability the land of the colony was divided into shares of twenty acres each, every "Purchaser" having one share in addition to the land he already possessed, and the heads of households to have as many shares, and therefore as many liabilities, as they had persons in their families. Strips of land along the riverside, five acres by four, were marked out for planting, and assigned by lot. The meadowland however was not to be divided, but held in common, except for haymaking when each person had assigned him a certain portion which he had liberty to mow.

It is interesting to know that it was not until 1624 that the colonists had any horned cattle, and the following year the four they had only increased to nine. In 1627 there were twelve cows which were divided among the 156 colonists, 57 men, 34 boys, 29 mothers, 36 girls and servants. Each group of thirteen persons had a cow which was allotted to them for ten years, after which the animal was returned to the common stock, with half her increase. The cattle, like the land, was assigned by lot to each of the divisions. Sometimes they bought out their partners as Miles Standish did, and thus obtained sole use of the cow for the remainder of the period.

All of this arrangement is most methodically recorded, which enables us to see where the colony actually stood at the end of the seven years, dating from the landing of the *Mayflower* in 1620. Taking all those who had at various times come to the colony, adding to the number those who had been born, they came altogether to 267. Of these 58 had died, 53 had gone elsewhere. It is a clear indication of the fearful hardships of the first year that we find in that year no fewer than 52 people died, whereas in the six remaining years only six had died. Not only does there remain this evidence of the growth of the colony from within but also an account of it as seen by those outside.

The Dutch connection

It will be remembered that in 1620 negotiations were carried on between the Dutch Merchants and the Pilgrim Fathers in Leyden, with a view to a settlement on the Hudson River. Three years later, in 1623, a permanent Dutch settlement was established at Manhattan, the present New York, but no contact took place between this settlement and Plymouth for several years. In March 1627, however, Bradford, as governor, received a friendly letter from Isaac de Rosier, the secretary of the colony at Manhattan. He suggested the establishment of contact between them which would be a help to each other, especially trade relationships. The Pilgrim Fathers replied that they were very ready to trade with them and, it is interesting to note that their reply was written in

Dutch, and that they apologised for their rude and imperfect writing of that language, offering the reason that they had not used it much recently. As a result of this correspondence the secretary visited the Pilgrim Fathers, and was received cordially and with due ceremony. He stayed long enough to spend a Sabbath with them and attend their services and departed having established trading relationships between their two colonies. It transpires that de Rosier later wrote a detailed and very favourable description of what he had seen at New Plymouth, and this letter found its way to the Royal Library in Holland in 1847, and has since been printed.

CHAPTER 7

The Second Exodus - Massachusetts

The idea of a second exodus of Puritans from
Lincolnshire to America began about 1627. In that
year Thomas Dudley knew "of some friends being
together in Lincolnshire, falling into discourse about
New England and the planting of the gospel there".
Out of this small beginning came the concept and
inception of the settlements around Massachusetts
Bay, New England. In so far as the Pilgrim Fathers
were pioneers, they have stood out as the vanguard of
the New England settlers. But in the degree of
importance, the second exodus was more vital in the
establishment of the New England Colonies. The
Pilgrim Fathers were few in number in face of the
Indians, Dutch and French settlers, all of whom were
in the North American continent at this time. Now in
the years 1628-1640, the years of the persecution of

Archbishop Laud and Charles I in England, a large cross-section of Englishmen, rich and poor, able and less able, crossed the Atlantic in search of freedom of worship. Before this movement slowed down over ninety University-educated men from Oxford and Cambridge (three-quarters from Cambridge) had gone out. Also about two-thirds of these men came from the eastern counties, with about one sixth from Devon, Dorset and Somerset, and the remainder from other parts of England.

So it is not unexpected that the name of the chief city of New England should be Boston and that the earliest counties of Massachusetts were Norfolk, Suffolk and Essex. Among the men who were famous as leaders of this exodus were John Winthrop of Groton Manor House, Lincolnshire and the Earl of Lincoln with his two houses, Sempringham Manor and Tattershall Castle. Lord Lincoln, a staunch Protestant, had gone to the Tower in 1627 for refusing to pay taxes illegally levied by Charles I, after Charles had tried to govern without Parliament. Among others who refused to pay these illegal taxes was Thomas Dudley.

Other Puritans like Roger Williams and Thomas Cotton speak of gatherings at Sempringham. Cotton was minister at Boston parish church; Thomas Dudley was Lord Lincoln's steward and confidential adviser. Lincoln never went himself to New England, but two of his sisters, Susan wife of John Humphreys and Arbella wife of Isaac Johnson both went out. The times were serious as Civil War was approaching.

Men like Oliver Cromwell, M.P. for Cambridge, were being raised up of the Lord to defend the rights and liberties of godly folk against the persecution of Arminian ritualists. Archbishop Laud was plotting to turn the Puritans out of the Church of England and turn back the tide of the Protestant Reformation. In the year 1628 "The Petition of Right" was presented to Charles I by Parliament. It was at this very time that the second exodus began and went on until the Long Parliament met in 1640, when the King began to give way in some measure to the demands of the people for civil and religious liberty.

Men of the second exodus

The men of the second exodus were not Separatists by conviction like the Pilgrim Fathers. They were Puritans in doctrine, conforming Churchmen, loyal in their attachment to the Church of England. Thus Francis Higginson, the Anglican minister who went out in 1629, when off Land's End called his family to look for the last time on the land they so loved. He said, "We will not say, as the Separatists were wont to say at their leaving of England, 'Farewell dear England, farewell Church of England,' though we cannot but separate from the corruptions in it; but we go to practise the positive part of church Reformation and propagate the gospel in America." John Winthrop and the company who sailed with him in 1630, when on board the *Arbella* east of Yarmouth, sent a humble request "to the rest of their brethren in and of the Church of England, for the obtaining of their prayers".

They went out from their country and the Church of England "with much sadness of heart and many tears".

The men of Lincolnshire, who in 1627 "fell into discourse about New England" took positive action. They first entered into correspondence with men of similar views in London and the west country. Those in the west lived principally around Dorchester. From this town in 1623 and onwards a private company of merchants had sent out fishing boats each year to the North American coast near Kennebec, and had tried and failed to establish a permanent settlement near Cape Ann. John White, the Puritan rector of Dorchester, saw in the failure of the Dorchester merchants the possibility of establishing a colony in New England for different reasons, and it is possible that it was a letter of his which started the conversations in Lincolnshire in 1627. When in 1626 the colony at Cape Ann was abandoned by the Dorchester merchants, some settlers moved fifteen miles to the south-west to the Indian village of Naumkeag, now known as Salem. Some of the merchants still felt that a settlement would succeed if more came out from England and brought cattle with them.

As the matter was discussed in London and the west, offers of funds were made if suitable emigrants were found willing to go. In the course of these inquiries John Endicott came forward as willing to accept the offer and go out. He was a native of Dorchester born there in 1588, a man of strong Puritan convictions, who had sat under the preaching of

Samuel Skelton, one of the ministers who went out in 1629. With John Endicott as leader a Patent was obtained from the Council of New England, dated 19th March, 1628, by which the Council sold to "some knights and gentlemen around Dorchester, namely Sir Henry Roswell, Sir John Young, Samuel Southcoat, John Humphrey, John Endicott and Simon Whitcomb, that part of New England lying between the Merrimac River and the Charles River on the Massachusetts Bay". The first expedition set sail on 20th June, 1628 from Weymouth in the ship *Abigail*, led by Endicott, and arrived at Naumkeag on 6th September. Together with Charles Gott, Richard Brackenburg and Richard Davenport, Endicott was entrusted by the Company at home with command until they themselves should follow.

Like the Pilgrim Fathers eight years earlier, these new settlers were taken sick in large numbers and many died. Endicott sent to the Pilgrim Fathers to Governor Bradford for their doctor, a deacon of their church, Samuel Fuller, who came over to help cure the sick. This kindly act established a firm bond of union between the settlements at Plymouth and at Naumkeag. Writing to Governor Bradford on 11th May, 1629, Endicott said, "I acknowledge myself much bound to you for your love and care in sending Mr. Fuller among us and rejoice much that I am by him satisfied touching your judgments of the outward form of God's worship. It is as far as I can gather no other than is warranted by the evidence of the truth and the same which I have professed and maintained ever since the Lord in mercy revealed Himself to me; being far from the common report that hath been spread of you as touching that particular."

Not only did Fuller help the sick but he also removed prejudices against the worship and practices of the Pilgrim Fathers which the men of "the second exodus" had brought out with them. Endicott was set on closer relations still. In the same letter to Governor Bradford he wrote, "It is a thing not unusual, that servants to one master and of the same household should be strangers. I assure you I desire it not, nay to speak more plainly, I cannot be so to you. God's people are all marked with one and the same mark, and sealed with one and the same seal, and have for the main, one and the same heart, guided by one and the same Spirit of truth; and where this is, there can be no discord nay, here must needs be sweet harmony. And the same request, I make unto the Lord, that we may, as Christian brethren, be united by a heavenly and unfeigned love; bending all our hearts and forces in furthering a work beyond our strength with reverence and fear, fastening our eyes always on Him that only is able to direct and prosper our ways."

A Royal Charter

As a close union grew up between the Salem and Plymouth settlers so the movement grew stronger back in the home country. Endicott sent back a good report of the country and his voyage and soon able and godly men in England began to consider helping the enterprise or going out to Salem. Among these was

John Winthrop, Isaac Johnson (brother-in-law of the Earl of Lincoln), Matthew Cradock a London merchant (later M.P. in the Long Parliament), Thomas Goff and Sir Richard Saltonstall. These men bought for the emigrants their right and interest in Massachusetts by a deed dated 19th March, 1628. They also went further than obtaining right of a private trading company when they obtained a Royal Charter dated 4th March, 1629, making the Company a legal Corporation under the title "The Governor and Company of the Massachusetts Bay in New England".

This Corporation in London was to annually elect a governor, deputy governor and eighteen assistants and to hold monthly meetings and general meetings four times a year. Matthew Cradock was elected governor and after his election it was agreed to create a second government, resident in the new colony, consisting of a governor, deputy and twelve councillors. This government was to be free from control of the governing body at home, thus foreseeing the time, it was hoped, when the Company at home would merge with the government in the colony. Each shareholder in the Company on payment of £50 would own 200 acres in the colony and if he went out and settled he would have 50 acres more for himself and 50 for each member of his family. Emigrants who were not shareholders were to be given 50 acres and 50 extra for each servant brought out.

In a letter dated 17th April, 1629, regarding the spiritual welfare of the colony, a member of the Company wrote, "For that the propagation of the gospel is a thing we do profess above all to be our aim in settling this plantation, we have been careful to make plentiful provision of godly ministers, by whose faithful preaching, godly conversation and exemplary life we trust not only those of our own nation will be built up in the knowledge of God, but also the Indians may in God's appointed time be reduced to the obedience of the gospel of Christ."

The three ministers sent out first were Samuel Skelton, a friend of John Endicott, Francis Higginson of Leicester and Francis Bright of Rayleigh in Essex. The London Company ordered Endicott to build them homes and provide all necessary things for their use. Not much is known of Skelton and Bright, but more information exists about Higginson. He was a noted Puritan preacher who had incurred the anger of the Laudian party because of the large congregations he drew in Leicester which had eventually made them eject him from his living. When he left Leicester for New England the Leicester people flocked the streets and "with prayers and tears" bade him farewell.

1629 - Five ships go to Massachusetts

Five vessels were to take Francis Higginson and the party sailing with him to America. They left London in April and May 1629. There was the *Talbot,* a ship of 300 tons carrying a hundred settlers and provisions for a year; the *George*, 300 tons with fifty-two settlers and provisions; the *Lion's Whelp*, 120 tons carrying many sailors and about forty settlers, especially from the Dorchester area; the *Four Sisters*,

300 tons carrying passengers, cattle and provisions, and finally the *Mayflower* which had been involved with the settlement of Plymouth Plantation and was now being used for the Massachusetts Bay colony.

The governor and Massachusetts Bay Company were much more generous with equipment than the Merchant Adventurers had been with the Plymouth settlers. They had learnt from the sad experiences of the first colony. Large supplies of clothing were now being sent out, including 200 suits, doublets, and hose of leather; 100 suits of northern "dussens" or Hampshire kerseys lined, the hose with skins, the doublets with linen of Guildford or "Gedlyman" serges; 300 plain falling bands such as had taken the place of the great ruffs of Elizabeth's time; 100 waistcoats of green cotton bound with red tape; 100 Monmouth capes and 100 leather girdles besides hooks and eyes for "mandflions", these being garments large and full of folds, with which "against cold nights the soldiers did use to wrap".

Besides these quaint and picturesque 17th- century garments, the ships carried food for the voyage and seeds and cereals for use when they got there, together with a supply of Spanish, Malaga and Canary wine. Also on board were horses, cattle, fishing nets, shotguns and also military equipment such as drums, ensigns, swords, corselets, pikes, muskets, small cannon with stores of powder and shot. As men were of more importance than material the Company had made certain that this expedition carried experienced craftsmen; those who could make pitch and salt, who could plant vines, (William Sherman was allowed 14 days before the ships sailed to fetch his vines from Northampton), men skilled in working iron and a surgeon and barber-surgeon; also Thomas Graves of Gravesend who professed to be skilled in the discovery of mines of all sorts, iron, lead, copper, and salt; in designing fortifications, in surveying buildings, measuring land and making maps (a good description of a present day general surveyor). The Company commanded Endicott the governor to take the advice of Graves in deciding where it would be best to settle, fortify and build a town.

With this equipment and experienced men, there went "many discreet, religious and well-ordered persons to be set over the rest dividing them into families, placing some with the ministers and others under such honest men as shall see them well educated in their general callings as Christians and according to their several trades". The Company was well aware that in such a large organisation, in spite of all their care, there could be trouble-makers and dishonest people. If any such were found the Company gave instructions that they were to be disciplined and if necessary sent back in the *Lion's Whelp* when she returned to England. Also the Company added, "Above all, we pray you be careful that there be none in our precincts permitted to do any injury in the least kind to the heathen people; and if any offend in that way let them receive due correction."

If the Indians claimed rights to any land then the Company directed their settlers "to purchase the title".

The Company gave instructions for the keeping of the Sabbath. Work in the colony was to cease every Saturday afternoon at 3 p.m. and the rest of the day was to be spent in preparation for the Sabbath as the ministers shall direct. Lambert Wilson the surgeon was to remain in the service of the settlers for three years and attend to the illnesses not only of the settlers but also of the Indians. He was also to train one or more young men suitable to succeed him in his profession.

One of these was to be the son of Francis Higginson the Leicester minister, if his father agreed, since he had been educated at the Leicester Grammar School before coming to the new colony. Everything showed from these instructions and arrangements made for this major expedition of 1629, that the men of the Company in London had learnt valuable lessons from the mistakes made by the Merchant Adventurers and the Pilgrim Fathers ten years before. All these instructions were contained in a general letter dated 17th April, 1629 directed to the settlers.

With this letter went a further letter dated 21st April, 1629 written at Gravesend while the ships waited there. In this the Company charged the settlers that special care be taken that family prayer be observed morning and evening and a watchful eye be had on all in each family so that trouble could be nipped in the bud. They thought it well to begin well. Their desire was for a kindly authority; but if any disorder arose then they believed correction was ordained for a fool's back, otherwise if there was no order in a family then there could be none in the new colony. Finally they wrote, "We heartily pray that all be kept to labour as the only means to reduce them to civil, yea, a godly life, and to keep youth from falling into many enormities which by nature we are all too much inclined to. God who alone is able and powerful, enable you to this great work and grant that our chiefest aim may be to His honour and glory."

Thus equipped and instructed those who went out in 1629 set forth; in the *George* about the middle of April, the *Talbot* and *Lion's Whelp* hoisting sail at Gravesend on the morning of 25th April, the *Four Sisters* and *Mayflower* following three weeks later. Francis Higginson who sailed in the *Talbot* kept a journal in which he described the experiences, sights and scenes of an Atlantic crossing. The captain and his crew every night set their eight and twelve o'clock watches singing a psalm and "a prayer that was not read out of a book". Morning and evening were marked by reading and expounding a chapter, singing and prayer. Preaching services took place twice on the Sabbath.

In times of great need "two solemn fasts were observed with great effect". Gazing on the angry seas, its mighty waves and equally majestic calm, Higginson wrote, "Those that love their own chimney corner, and dare not go beyond their own town's end, shall never have the honour to see the wonderful works of the Almighty God." Writing back in September to old friends in Leicester, who were purposing to come out to join the settlement,

Higginson advised them what to bring for use on the voyage and in the colony. He said, "When you are once parted from England you shall meet with neither taverns nor alehouses, nor butcher, nor grocer, nor apothecary (chemist) nor shops to help what things you need in the midst of the great ocean, nor when you are come to land; here are neither markets nor fairs to buy what you want."

1629 - The colonists reach Massachusetts

On arriving at Salem, Massachusetts the three ministers entered into discussions with Endicott and other godly people as to the type of church they wanted in the colony, stating for themselves that they wanted a Reformed congregation. These were church principles similar to those in operation at Plymouth Plantation. Higginson and Skelton agreed with this idea, while Bright dissented and eventually left and went to Charlestown. Three weeks after their arrival a solemn day of fasting and prayer was set apart for the choice of a pastor and teacher.

Ministers ordained

The day opened with prayer; then Higginson and Skelton answered various questions about their views on the calling of a minister. Their replies were twofold: first the inward call, or God's calling by which the man was endowed with the necessary gifts and his heart moved to desire the work; next the outward call which comes from God's people, when a company of believers are joined together in covenant to walk together in the ways of God, and when the men thus gathered have a free voice in the choice of their officers. These views being accepted with men only voting, the pastor and teacher were chosen by a paper ballot, as a result of which Skelton was chosen as pastor, and Higginson as teacher.

The difference between the two is explained by John Eliot when he says, "Mr Skelton being farther advanced in years was constituted as pastor of the Salem Church, Mr. Higginson, the teacher." The difference in the office was therefore one of seniority. Then the service continued after prayer had been made for the two ministers, "First Mr. Higginson with three or four of the gravest members of the church laid their hands on Mr. Skelton using prayer therewith. This being done there was imposition of hands on Mr. Higginson also." Charles Gott, one of those who came to Salem with Endicott in 1628, wrote to governor Bradford an account of the service of ordination which had taken place on 20th July. In his letter he said, "And now, good sir, I hope that you and the rest of God's people (who are acquainted with the ways of God) with you, will say that here was a right foundation laid, and that these blessed servants of the Lord came in at the door and not at the window."

The Salem Covenant

Later on August 6th a day was observed for fasting and prayer, when both ministers preached and towards the end of the day the *Confession and Covenant* of the Salem church was solemnly read and assented to.

Morton in his *Memorial* says that governor Bradford
and some members of Plymouth Plantation were
present either at the ordination or at the day of fasting.
Morton says that governor Bradford and his company
coming by sea, were delayed by cross winds, and so
could not be there at the beginning of the day. But they
came into the assembly afterward, and gave them the
right hand of fellowship, wishing all prosperity and all
blessedness to such good beginnings. From this it
seems that the godly governor was probably present at
the fast day on August 6th.

In the *Salem Covenant* the church covenanted
'with the Lord and with one another to walk together
in all His ways so far as He revealed Himself to them
in His Word, and this through the power and grace of
the Lord Jesus Christ; avouching the Lord to be their
God, and themselves to be His people in the truth and
simplicity of their spirits; to give themselves to the
Lord Jesus Christ to be governed by Him, resolving to
cleave unto Him alone for life and glory, and to reject
all contrary ways, canons and constitutions of men in
His worship; to walk with their brethren in all
brotherliness, avoiding jealousy, suspicion and
censure; to avoid all occasions of dishonouring Christ
in the church; to study the advancement of the gospel
in all truth and peace, not slighting sister churches but
taking counsel of them as need shall be; to carry
themselves in all lawful obedience to those that are
over them in Church and commonwealth; to approve
themselves to the Lord in their worldly callings,
shunning idleness as the bane of any state, and not to

deal hardly or oppressively with any; and finally, promising to the best of their ability to teach their children and servants the knowledge of God and of His will that they may serve Him also.'

This *Covenant* accepted that day was renewed on special occasions from time to time. It was also used when new members were received into the church, giving their experience and assenting to this *Covenant.* The whole of this expedition and settlement of 1629 shows a movement very akin to later Nonconformity, especially among Particular Baptists in England in the 17th and 18th centuries. It is the more interesting when it is realised that these godly men in their own estimation still remained loyal members of that one church they knew, the Church of England.

CHAPTER 8

First Principles

Disagreements

The *Covenant* and church order thus agreed did not however meet with unanimous approval. Francis Bright, one of the three ministers who had come out, left Salem and went to Charlestown, and two members of the Council, John and Samuel Browne, leading members of the party, openly expressed their dissatisfaction that the ministers did not use the *Book of Common Prayer,* did not administer the ordinances of baptism and the Lord's Supper with the ceremonies usually observed in England. Also the ministers had expressed their intention of denying admission to the Lord's Table of people they considered not fit to come to it. Going from protest to action, they gathered a company for worship separate from the main assembly conducting their service according to the *Book of Common Prayer.*

Endicott the governor, seeing the confusion that was growing, called the two brothers to meet him. In the course of the discussion they charged the two ministers, Skelton and Higginson, with departing from the order of the Church of England and with being Separatists like the Pilgrim Fathers. If the two continued in this way they would end up as Anabaptists. The ministers replied that they were neither Separatists nor Anabaptists, that they were not separating from the Church of England, or from the ordinances of God in her midst, but only from the corruptions and disorders which had sprung up in that Church in recent years. They had come away from their native land, they said, after suffering much on behalf of their convictions, that they might get away from the *Prayer Book* and the ceremonies, and being now in a place where they could have their liberties, they had no intention of using the *Book of Common Prayer* or its ceremonies, as they considered that they were a sinful corruption of the worship of God imposed on them by King and bishops.

The governor and Council having considered the answers, and sounded out the whole company that had come out, agreed with Skelton and Higginson that they were still members of the Church of England while not using the *Book of Common Prayer* and its ceremonies. But John and Samuel Browne remained firm in their belief that all members of the Church of England must of necessity, to remain members, use the *Book of Common Prayer*. Seeing that this would radically divide the colony and separate the whole company,

Endicott and the Council decided that the only way of dealing with the problem was to send the two brothers back to England. This they did in the same year.

Intolerance

The action of Endicott and his Council at Massachusetts regarding John and Samuel Browne was the same as that taken by the Pilgrim Fathers at Plymouth in regard to Byford and Oldham. In later years in Massachusetts governor Winthrop had to take similar action. Such action has called down on their heads the charge of intolerance from later generations of historians. Such action has appeared as grossly inconsistent on the part of men who themselves had fled from intolerance at home. In assessing the situation, one thing is clear. Had they allowed a group of people to remain in the colony who might be ready to offer a helping hand to any repressive measures that could be taken against them by the government of Charles I, then they could lose the liberty they had already acquired to worship as they wished.

It must also be understood that in the 17th century religious toleration as we know it today in this country was not accepted anywhere in Europe. One religion, one state [una civitas, una religio], that is an established religion in each state which was by law required to be the religion of every individual citizen, was the accepted practice of the day. As late as 1687 Particular Baptists in England were fined for not attending the Church of England and Presbyterians were hounded over the moors of Scotland for the same reason.

As Endicott and his Council saw it, the question was not whether to tolerate John and Samuel Browne and their group, but whether, as more and more emigrants came out from England, they might find themselves in a minority, being forced by the Browne group's intolerance to leave Massachusetts and seek liberty elsewhere in America. All they could see was that the dissenting group was very loyal to the Church of England and its ceremonies. In their minds this meant Archbishop Laud and Charles I and their policy of persecution against Puritans.

In this light it is easier to understand their very real fear. The intolerance they had come from had been that of a strong government turning out of their native land a community of Puritans who disagreed with the ceremonies of the Established Church. In New England the intolerance was that of the same community of Puritans concerned to guard the liberty which had cost so much. This liberty might easily have been taken from them by infiltration of people, placed there by the government of Charles I, to cause divisions among them, a situation which developed at Plymouth among the Pilgrim Fathers.

Nonetheless, having said all this, it is a sad comment that they still found themselves in a position where wisdom dictated a degree of intolerance on their part. In England in the 17th century very few understood what toleration meant; one of the outstanding men who desired it, and tried to produce it, but failed to obtain it in any great degree or for long was Oliver Cromwell.

The Reformed Faith in Massachusetts

On the surface it seems strangely inconsistent that Endicott and those who went with him in 1628, and Skelton and Higginson and those who went with them in 1629, and looking ahead for a moment, Winthrop and those who went with him in 1630, while expressing such affection for the Church of England, when they left their home country, should have made such fundamental changes in the Church services. The explanation is not entirely to be found in their having come into close contact with the Separatists of Plymouth colony. John Cotton, who went out in 1634 to Massachusetts, speaking of the church at Salem as organised under Endicott, Skelton and Higginson, writes, "How far they of Salem take up any practice from Plymouth I do not know. Sure I am that Mr. Skelton was studious of that way before he left Lincolnshire. Those who really know these men and their spirit will discern easily that they are not such as will be leavened by vicinity of neighbours, but by the divinity of the truth of God shining forth from the Word."

The real explanation however lies deeper. The men themselves in making the changes never for a moment considered that they had ceased to be Church of England men. In writing back to friends at home they admitted that in going abroad they had begun to search and try their ways. In doing this, they had found that they came to see that some things which at the beginning of their ministry had not greatly concerned them, or they had practised without much thought, when weighed in the balances of the sanctuary, they found had not sufficient warrant from Scripture to justify them being retained in the new country.

The question of the government of the Church by bishops was historically for them, in the period since the Reformation, a relatively new thing. In the early part of the reign of Queen Elizabeth I, prominent bishops of the Church of England had had close friendships with some of the Swiss Reformers. Until the time of Archbishop Laud, in the reign of Charles I, the concept of the divine right of bishops through the apostolic succession, and therefore the divine ordination of clergy by them, had not arisen. Such an idea was, of course, the accepted tradition of Roman Catholics.

To most clergy in England, the authority of a bishop derived solely from his appointment by the Monarch under an Act of Parliament passed at the time of the Reformation in the reign of Henry VIII. Only High Church Anglicans took up the position that the church could not exist without the appointment of bishops. When Laud, as a young man, took his degree at Oxford, and took up the idea of the apostolic succession in the appointment of bishops, Dr. Holland, the Regius Professor of Divinity, referred to him "as one that did cast a bone of discord betwixt the Church of England and the Reformed Churches beyond the seas", and Laud's thesis was denounced as "a novel Popish position".

As with the question of the government of the Church by bishops, so with the use of the *Prayer Book*, the wearing of the surplice and the practice of various ceremonies, the men of Massachusetts contended that these were still open questions, and the views they held were more in accordance with the principles of the Reformation than were the views of John and Samuel Browne and their followers; that *they* were in fact the true representatives of the National Reformed Church of England. It must be noted however that Skelton and Higginson had adopted two principles in relation to Church life which carried them further in the direction of Separatism than they themselves were aware. Even in his Leicester days, Francis Higginson had exercised a discipline of his own at Communion in refusing to allow immoral persons to partake; he did not regard it as the right of every parishioner who had been baptised in infancy to come to Communion.

In New England Higginson and Skelton went a stage further when they acknowledged, "We receive to our churches only visible saints and believers; in common with many good men we desire all separation of the precious from the vile. This day hath discovered what kind of people are to be found everywhere in the parishes of England. Can light and darkness, Christ and Belial agree together? Popish and episcopal enemies cleave together in our church of Christ with the saints of God."

The second principle which carried them further in the direction of Separatism than they realised stemmed from the first. It was as they put it, "giving discipline as well as other ordinances to particular churches, not subjecting them to any government out of themselves, but only to take the brotherly counsel and help of one another". "If", they said, "the Church be pure and have such officers as the New Testament requires, we need not fear to betrust the Church with that power which we conceive Christ hath given to the same, other Churches watching over them and counselling them in the Lord. The reforming the material of a Church, and the recalling of the power of government to the Church, tends much to further the work of the Reformation and in no way hinders the same."

Thus while they protested they were not Separatists, but sincere members of the Church of England, they had adopted the two main principles on which Separatism was based; namely that to be true members of a Christian church evidence must be shown of the work of the Holy Spirit in the heart, the new birth; secondly that churches composed of such believers were capable of self-government and needed no bishop or Presbyterian Synod to oversee them or appoint their ministers without consulting them.

The difference between the men of Salem and the men of Plymouth was that the former retained the State Church principle in spirit, while the latter did not. Into the *Salem Confession* Francis Higginson had put a clause about "the duty and power of the magistrate in matters of religion". To secure the best laws they gave the right to vote only to men of consistent character and members of the church. Church membership thus became the qualification for citizens' rights, and the churches came under the supervision of the civic authority. This was a similar situation to that of Calvin at Geneva, and was sadly open to produce much trouble, for persons who were disciplined by the church and removed from membership also lost their right to vote for the Council of the colony. The colonists can hardly be blamed if in founding a new Christian community they created situations which would produce trouble in days to come.

In all they did in Massachusetts, Endicott, Skelton and Higginson did what they felt was best. Higginson wrote, "We might have remained in England and found a way to fill the prisons, but whether we were called to that when there was an open door of liberty placed before us, we leave to be considered. The Lord Himself knew the motives which animated us in going abroad. He, that seeth in secret and rewardeth openly, knew what prayers and tears had been poured out to God, by many alone, and in days of fasting and prayer, by God's servants together for His counsel, direction and blessing in this work. Many longings and pantings of heart had there been in many after the Lord Jesus to see His goings in the sanctuary; and this liberty of New England, we have looked upon and thankfully received from God, as the fruit of these prayers and desires."

The Massachusetts settlers of 1630

In 1628 and 1629 two groups of settlers had gone out to Massachusetts; a still larger group was to follow in 1630. But an important decision had to be taken before this group left England. Those who composed the Massachusetts Bay Company were not content to remain a trading company with their headquarters in London, open at any time to the interference of the government of Charles I. They had a vision of a free state across the seas having its own self-government. But it was difficult to achieve this under the watchful eye of Charles I and Archbishop Laud.

The difficulty was overcome by a resolution passed at a meeting of the General Court of the Company held on 28th July, 1629, when the governor, Matthew Cradock, suggested that in order to induce people of character and rank to go out to the colony, and for other weighty reasons not mentioned but perfectly well understood, it was necessary "to transfer the government of the colony to those that shall inhabit it, and not to continue the same in subordination to the Company here as it is". This matter was left to the next meeting, to be kept strictly confidential.

Self-government for Massachusetts

Before the next meeting, however, Sir Richard Saltonstall, John Winthrop, Thomas Dudley, Isaac Johnson and eight other governors met privately at Cambridge and bound themselves by written agreement, "on the word of a Christian and in the presence of God, who is the searcher of all hearts", that they would be ready by 1st March, 1630, to leave with their families for the colony, provided that by the end of September the whole government of the colony shall be vested in the hands of those who live there. This was agreed on 26th August, 1629, and three days later at a formal court of the governors the matter was agreed by general consent. The practical result of this was to place the entire control of the Company in the hands of those ten members of the Company who were going out themselves to the colony.

As the existing governor, Matthew Cradock, was not going, it was necessary to choose a new governor who was. At a Court held on October 20th, 1629, John Winthrop was "with a general vote and full consent" chosen to be governor of the Company for the next year, beginning from that date. This election of their governor was fully justified, for Winthrop was elected governor again on no fewer than eleven occasions in the history of the colony.

CHAPTER 9

The 1630 Emigrants

Governor Winthrop

"Governor Winthrop is one of the great names in American history, taking his place with that of George Washington himself." (*Pilgrim Fathers of New England.* John Brown. Page 283). Descended from an ancient and honourable family in Suffolk, he was born at Groton Manor House, near Sudbury, in 1588. He was trained to the Law, was a member of the Inner Temple and at a later date was one of the attorneys of the Court of Wards and Liveries. He was a typical example of a godly Puritan, grave, earnest, hardworking, and a gentleman. He had a nature inclined to seriousness; it had been further weighted by the sorrows of life. When only twenty-eight, he was for the second time left a widower with six children. His third marriage with Margaret Tyndal in 1618 was made a great blessing to him, and brought back to his home some of the joy of life, at a time when he had been so saddened.

Winthrop's spiritual experience

He says about his own spiritual experience that when only ten he had some notions about God, prayed to Him in danger and "found manifest answer". "At about twelve," he says, he "began to have some more savour of religion." When eighteen, under the ministry of Ezekiel Culverwell "the word came home to him with power, he having found only light before". Now he came "to some peace and comfort in God and in His ways; loved a Christian and the very ground he trod on; honoured a faithful minister in his heart and could have kissed his feet; had an insatiable thirst for the word of God, and could not miss a good sermon though many miles off, especially of such as did search deep into the conscience."

Thus he goes on: "Now could my soul close with Christ and rest there with sweet content, so ravished with His love as that I desired nothing nor feared anything, but was filled with joy unspeakable and glorious, and with a spirit of adoption could now cry, 'My Father,' with more confidence. When riding along the country roads to London it pleased God that I now made great use of my time, both in praying, singing and meditating with good intention and much comfort: my meditation being often as to how the Spirit of God reveals the love of God to us and causeth us to love Him again; how He unites all the faithful in deed and in affection; how He opens our understanding in the mysteries of the Gospel and makes us believe and obey. I found great sweetness therein, it shortened my way and lightened all such troubles and difficulties as I was wont to meet with."

Winthrop in times of persecution

As the Government of Charles I and Archbishop Laud began their unconstitutional regime, and harassed people for refusal to pay unparliamentary taxes, or to succumb to High Anglican ritual imposed on all citizens, Winthrop began to fear for his country and to consider leaving it. In the spring of 1629 he wrote to his wife: "The Lord has admonished, threatened, corrected and astonished us, yet we grow worse and worse. He hath smitten all the other Churches before our eyes, and hath made them drink of the bitter cup of tribulation even unto death. We saw this and humbled not ourselves to turn from our evil ways ... I am verily persuaded God will bring some heavy affliction upon this land, and that speedily. Yet He will not forsake us; though He correct us with the rods of men, yet if He take not His mercy and lovingkindness from us we shall be safe. He only is all-sufficient; if we have Him, we have all things."

Also for economic reasons, Winthrop was of the opinion that emigration had become a necessity. Even in those days men were talking of surplus population in England. Winthrop writes: "This land grows weary of her inhabitants so as man who is most precious of all creatures is here more vile and base than the earth we tread upon, and of less price among us than a horse or a sheep ... We use the authority of Law to hinder the increase of the people as by urging a statute against cottages and inmates; and thus it has come to pass that children, servants and neighbours, especially if they be poor, are counted the greatest burdens, which, if things were right, they would be the chiefest earthly blessings. The whole earth is the Lord's garden and He hath given it to the sons of men ... why, then, should we stand striving here for places of habitation and in the meantime suffer a whole continent, as fruitful and convenient for the use of man, to lie waste without any improvement?"

There were not wanting those at home who wished to see men of the calibre of John Winthrop stay in England. His neighbour in Suffolk, Robert Ryece, wrote to him on 12th August, 1629, saying, "The Church and Commonwealth here at home hath more need of your best ability in these dangerous times than any remote plantation." But the letter came too late. In John Winthrop's diary for 28th July, 1629, there is the following entry: "My brother Downing and myself, riding into Lincolnshire by Ely, my horse fell under me in a bog in the fens, so that I was almost to the waist in water; but the Lord preserved me from further danger, blessed be His name."

This ride into Lincolnshire meant that he had been to Sempringham or Tattershall Castle in earnest conference with Isaac Johnson, John Humphrey, Thomas Dudley and others of the Boston men, about the New England scheme. On 26th August, 1629,

John Winthrop was one of the twelve who signed the solemn agreement entered into at Cambridge, and on 20th October he was chosen as the first governor to be resident in the colony. On 23rd March, 1630, he and his associates sailed from Southampton in four boats: the *Arbella*, the *Jewel*, the *Ambrose* and the *Talbot*. Two other boats preceded them in February and March, while ten others including the *Mayflower* followed in May and June. Landing at Yarmouth in the Isle of Wight on 7th April, they issued a document entitled "The humble request of his majesty's loyal subjects, to the rest of their brethren in the Church of England for the obtaining of their prayers, promising in return, so far as God shall enable us, to give Him no rest on your behalfs, wishing our heads and hearts may be fountains of tears for your everlasting welfare when we shall be in our poor cottages in the wilderness."

1630-Settlers arrive in Massachusetts

Leaving Yarmouth on 8th April and passing the Scilly Isles on the 11th, they reached America on 12th June. The following winter Thomas Dudley wrote to the Countess of Lincoln an account of their voyage and of what they saw when they landed. He can only do it rudely, he says, "having yet no table, nor other room to write in, than by the fireside upon my knee, in this sharp winter". Dudley went on to recount that seventeen ships had arrived safely in New England, and that the four in which Winthrop and his companions had sailed had made a long, troublesome and costly voyage, being all windbound at starting and hindered by contrary winds after they set sail, being scattered with mists and tempests so that few of them arrived together.

The Atlantic crossing

They had scarcely lost sight of the English coast when they had seen eight ships astern of them. When leaving Yarmouth they had been warned that ten French ships were waiting off the coast for them. Preparations were at once made for action. Lady Arbella and the other women and children were sent down to the lower deck to be out of danger. Gun room and gun deck were cleared, hammocks taken down, guns loaded, and every man was armed and sent to his station. "All things being thus fitted," says Dudley, "we went to prayer upon the upper deck. It was much to see how cheerful and comfortable all the company appeared; not a woman or a child that showed fear, though all did apprehend the danger to have been great. Our trust was in the Lord of Hosts and the courage of our captain who tacked about and stood to meet them."

It was a false alarm. The suspected enemy turned out to be friends; "so when we drew near, every ship as they met saluted each other, and so God be praised, our fear and danger was turned into mirth and friendly entertainment." The rest of their adventures were those fairly common to any Atlantic voyage. On the seventieth day out land was sighted on the seventy-second day "there came a smell of the shore like the smell of a garden" and on the seventy-sixth day, Saturday, 12th June, the *Arbella* came to anchor off the coast of New England. The Pilgrim Fathers had landed in the depths of winter; these their successors came in the height of summer and "most of our people went on shore upon the land of Cape Ann, which lay very near us, and gathered store of fine strawberries". Thus there arrived some of the men who were to be key figures in the political and spiritual development of the New England settlement.

Winthrop takes up his governorship

Winthrop, on landing at Salem, at once assumed office as governor of the colony. He had great responsibilities as about the time of his arrival a thousand people were added to the colony and soon afterwards another thousand, making the population between two and three thousand, with their own governor and governing assembly, engaged in erecting towns and villages. It was not only a time of development but also a time of much discouragement. "We found the colony", says Dudley, "in a sad and unexpected condition, about eighty of them being dead the winter before, and many of those alive being weak and sick, all the corn and bread amongst them hardly sufficient to feed them a fortnight." From the first Winthrop and his party had to feed the existing settlers as well as themselves from their own supplies. Winthrop came to be looked upon as the Joseph to whom all the people went when their own corn supplies failed. It is related that six months after his arrival, as he gave a poor man the last handful of meal from the barrel, a ship arrived in the harbour with fresh food supplies.

Winthrop and his companions found on their arrival that many of the reports about the colony they had received in the home country had been exaggerated. Dudley speaks of "too large commendations of the country and the commodities thereof". He says also, "Salem, when we landed, pleased us not." This led to further explorations about the bay, with the result that the settlers developed scattered towns and villages, some at Charlestown on the north side of the River Charles, others at Boston on the south side; others at Medford, Watertown, Roxbury and Dorchester. Winthrop himself settled first at Charlestown, but soon moved his new timber house across the river to Boston which became accepted as the main town of the colony. Within a year of their arrival there were no fewer than eight separate settlements along the shores of the bay from Salem to Dorchester, Watertown, five miles up the river from Charlestown, being the farthest settlement.

During the first year heavy sorrows came on them. Winthrop's own son, Henry, was accidentally drowned at Salem, and under the date 30th September the governor has this entry: "About two in the morning Mr. Isaac Johnson died; his wife, the Lady Arbella, of the house of Lincoln, being dead about one month before. He was a holy man and wise and died in sweet peace, leaving some part of his substance to the colony." Cotton Mather says of Lady Arbella, "She left an earthly paradise to encounter the sorrows of the wilderness for the entertainments of a pure worship in the house of God; and then left that wilderness for paradise, taking New England on her way to heaven." Earlier in the same month Francis Higginson had passed away to the great grief of the colonists, who valued his ministry; also William Gager "a right godly man, and skilful chirurgeon (doctor) and one of the deacons of the congregation".

Dudley estimated that of those who came over, no fewer than two hundred passed away between April and December 1630. Some also returned home, but the rest remained. Winthrop wrote to his wife: "The Lord is pleased still to humble us; yet He mixes so many mercies with His corrections, as we are persuaded He will not cast us off, but in His due time will do us good, according to the measure of our afflictions. He stays but until He hath purged our corruptions, healed the hardness and error of hearts, and stripped us of our vain confidence in this arm of flesh, that He may have us rely wholly upon Himself... We may not look at great things here. It is enough that we shall have heaven, though we should pass through hell to it. We here enjoy God and Jesus Christ. Is not this enough? I do not repent my coming; and if I were to come again, I would not have altered my course, though I had foreseen all these afflictions."

Government and defence of Massachusetts

As the settlement grew to be a state, various problems arose over the methods of government. At first government was through the General Court of the

Massachusetts Bay Company transferred to New England. Then in October 1630 the rights of government were transferred from this Court of freemen of the Company to the governor, deputy-governor and their assistants. Also the election of the governor was transferred from the Court of freemen to the governor's assistants. This put power in the hands of a few men around the governor.

The Watertown protest

In August 1630 there had been news that the French intended to attack the colony. Plans were made to erect fortifications on the frontier at Newtown and to pay for this a tax of £60 was levied on each of the various settlements by the governor and his assistants. When the levy came to be made on Watertown, the freemen there objected on the ground that no tax could be levied on them except by an assembly in which they were represented. (This was the very same reason why back in England men had refused to pay the Ship Money levied by Charles I at a time when he had suspended Parliament for over ten years and was governing by himself.)

When summoned to Boston these freemen gave in and paid, but they had made their point and manifested the spirit which was to appear in the next century in the American War of Independence, when the American Colonies refused to be taxed by the British Government at Westminster, an Assembly in which they had no representation. Also the point about representation was taken by the governor, his deputy and assistants, as in 1631 powers of government laid down that the Court of freemen should elect the governor, his deputy and assistants. It was also arranged that every town should send two representatives to advise the governor and his assistants on taxation. So the Watertown protest had some effect on establishing a more democratic form of government with more consultation.

Representative government

In 1634 the freemen of each town elected three representatives, who, twenty-four in number, presented themselves at the General Court of the governor and asked to see the Charter of the Company, maintaining that the right to elect officials and make laws was in their hands. While the governor did not at once agree, he finally accepted that they had full powers of election and legislation. Henceforth there were to be four Courts a year, at one of which the whole body of the freemen were to elect the governor, his deputy, and assistants. At the other three meetings the representatives of the various towns were to legislate, make grants of land, and transact other necessary public business.

In this way though there was not a vote for every man, yet in so far as representation was understood at home in the English Parliament when in session, the colonists of Massachusetts began to establish a representative form of government. At the same time another problem arose which was similar to the problem in the British Constitution regarding the respective powers exercised in government between the House of Commons and the House of Lords. This was the relationship between the governor and his assistants, and the deputies from the various towns. The powers of each had been largely undefined and at first they all sat together in one chamber, and discussed matters affecting the day-to-day government of the colony.

A balance of power

In 1634 the two groups came into conflict. On a particular issue twenty of the deputies voted in favour and five were against it; and of the governor and his assistants only two, including the governor, were in favour of it. At this moment arose the issue as to whether the consent of a majority of both groups was essential for the passing of any business, or whether a majority of the deputies overruled the opposition of the governor and his assistants. In fact in this matter with the governor himself and two of his assistants being in favour and agreeing with the majority of the deputies, the rest of the assistants gave way and by precedent power began to come to the deputies as a group.

Slowly as the colonists had sought religious freedom, so they began to feel their way to political freedom at a time when few understood how it could be achieved or maintained. In England, within a few years after these events in the colony, there was to be the Civil War between King and Parliament on this very issue of religious and political freedom, the right to be in both spheres a "nonconformist" or "dissenter" or "independent" or "separatist".

Church membership and the right to a vote

While freedom was slowly broadening in the colony in the political direction, it was however being narrowed in another direction. Having adopted, as mentioned previously, in church government the principle that only persons who could show a true work of the Holy Spirit in their hearts could be accepted as church members, the colonists then went on to decree that no man should be a freeman (and have a right to elect deputies) unless he were a member of the church in the colony. Then after church membership was made a necessary qualification for voting at town meetings and for the deputies, an Act was passed by the governor and deputies granting to the towns the right of dividing their lands, electing constables and surveyors and of enforcing their orders by a fine of twenty shillings.

In this way non-church members had no political rights, and yet absolute control of their secular affairs was given to men, whose one qualification was that they were church members. Here was a problem which the godly have always faced when in political power. In England Oliver Cromwell found the issue impossible when the Parliament of the "Saints" sat at Westminster, a body of men brought together because of their reputation for being godly persons. Twice at a later date Cromwell failed to re-establish parliamentary government in England and had to return to rule the country by the Army.

The main reason for his failure was that he saw a freely elected Parliament bent on removing him from government and returning to persecution of godly people. When the godly are in power politically and rule over the ungodly, there is bound to be a conflict and a great danger of injustice or intolerance. The seeds of bitterness were sown in the Massachusetts colony by church membership being made the qualification for voting; on the one hand it offered a very unworthy inducement to attempt to become a church member, and on the other hand it created an element of bitterness and discontent. While non - church members were not excluded from the colony, or freed from civic duties or the oath of allegiance to the government, yet they were not given the rights of a citizen.

Still, in spite of its difficulties, the Massachusetts colony prospered under its governor Winthrop, faced as he was with such complex political problems. By 1634 nearly four thousand Englishmen had come and about twenty villages had been founded on or near the shores of the bay. Permanent houses and bridges were erected; roads and fences made; farms were beginning to develop as was trade in such things as timber, furs and salted fish which were sent back to England. Political meetings were held, justice was administered by magistrates as in England and services were conducted by about twenty ministers, nearly all of whom had been ministers in the Church of England

and had been educated at Oxford and Cambridge Universities.

It has been estimated that between 1630 and 1639 the number of men trained in one of the English Universities, who had gone to Massachusetts, was between sixty and seventy, three-quarters of these remaining in the colony, and that by 1647 their number had increased to at least ninety. These men maintained standards of learning and provided many godly able ministers. Their influence was largely behind the foundation of the two great American Universities of Yale and Harvard.

CHAPTER 10

Spiritual Leaders

John Cotton

Not only were the leaders of the Massachusetts Colony men of university education, but also men of strong character. Beside Winthrop, Endicott and Johnson, foremost among these was John Cotton. He had been born at Derby in England in 1585. He entered Trinity College, Cambridge at the age of thirteen in 1598. He later moved to Emmanuel College where he became a Fellow and tutor. At the age of twenty-three he became well known through his sermon preached in Latin at the funeral of Dr. Some, Master of Peterhouse College. Like John Robinson, the minister of the Pilgrim Fathers in Holland, John Cotton was one of those Cambridge students who came under the powerful ministry of William Perkins, the great Puritan preacher of Cambridge, minister at St Mary's Church. He tried for a while to resist the conviction of sin which was wrought in his soul under Perkins' ministry. He feared that if he became a godly man it would ruin his career as a learned man. But the power of the Holy Spirit through the ministry of William Perkins was mightier than he, and after much deep soul exercise the Lord brought him out to be one of the most powerful and able ministers of his day.

Minister in Boston U.K.

In 1612 he became minister of St. Botolph's, the famous parish church of Boston in Lincolnshire, its tower a noted landmark in the area. From the very first his ministry was blessed to the people, and this did not pass the notice of the ecclesiastical authorities. In the records of Lincoln Cathedral there exists a manuscript which describes a tour of the diocese by Bishop Neile in 1614. In it are descriptions of the various parishes and their vicars. Among these accounts is that of a visit to Boston parish church. The record describes John Cotton as "a young man, but by report of great gravity and sanctity of life, a man of rare parts for his learning, eloquent and well spoken, ready upon a sudden, and very apprehensive (quick to grasp) to conceive of any point in learning though never so abstruse, insomuch that those his good gifts have won him so much credit and acceptance, not only with his parishioners at Boston, but with all the ministry and men of account in these quarters, that grave and learned men, out of an admiration of those good graces of God in him, have been, and upon every occasion still are, willing to submit their judgments to his in any point of controversy, as though he were some extraordinary Paraclete that could not err".

This is an interesting description considering that bishops as a whole had little time for Puritan clergy. The report goes on, "We heard three of his sermons in two days, which three were six hours long very near. The sermons were well conceived, were delivered modestly and soberly, and were well worthy of all commendation; but alas, nothing in this world is perfect: there was 'death in the pot'; every sermon to our judgment was poisoned with some error or other. In one sermon he maintained that the pagan world would not be condemned for want of belief in Christ, but only for moral transgressions against the law of nature written in their hearts; in another he contended that the office of apostle was extinct in the Church; that it was a flat error to think any man a lawful minister who was not a preacher; ordination did not make such a man a minister, though God's terrible providence might set him over His people in His anger and heavy displeasure, but not in mercy; he further taught that reading was not preaching; that non-residence (some clergy had more than one parish and some bishops were government ministers, so they were often absent from their parishes) was utterly unlawful; that it was not lawful to let the Sabbath pass without two sermons; and that by the order of deacons in the Bible was meant neither more nor less than collectors for the poor." (In the Church of England deacons are a type of junior minister.) It is clear from these remarks, that the Church authorities thought that John Cotton was a man who needed watching.

The report goes on, "His authors, he is most beholden to, are of the newest stamp." This revealing remark shows just how well the Puritan clergy were known to the bishops, and how they regarded them, men of "the newest stamp". The report concludes with a description of the Sunday services at Boston parish church. It says, "They have prayers with psalms after the lessons; after the second lesson a psalm is sung, which is followed by a sermon two hours long; then another psalm, after which the parish clerk calls out the children to be catechised, each one answering aloud as they used to do at a sessions, with a 'Here, Sir.' After this call there is a long prayer by the minister of the town, and then come the questions out of a catechism of his own making, and finally he spends two hours more in explanation of questions and answers; if they keep the same tenor all the year, their afternoon worship will be five hours long, where to our observation, there were as many sleepers as wakers, scarce any man but sometimes forced to wink and nod."

In the course of time complaints were lodged against Cotton in the Bishop's Court at Lincoln, and he was stopped from preaching but later allowed to continue. He was Vicar of Boston parish church for twenty years and openly taught many things that must have offended the bishop of his diocese. Among these things he believed that bishops should be only over one congregation, and that authority in the Church rested in the hands of each congregation, and there was no one superior to a minister and his congregation. He rested his beliefs on the Scriptures, and felt that it was the example the Lord had given to His Church.

What is even more striking is that in Boston Cotton set up a gathered Church, that is a group of godly people within his parish who entered into covenant with God and one another "to follow after the Lord in the purity of His worship". The fact that he was left at liberty while he had such views is difficult to understand. The Bishop of Lincoln, John Williams, appointed in 1621, favoured Puritan teaching, and was away from his diocese most of the time from 1621 to 1626, when he was Lord Keeper of the Privy Seal. This may help to explain why John Cotton preached unmolested for so long.

But the time was coming when the bishop would be forced to take some action in the case of Cotton. In 1625 he wrote to Cotton for an explanation of his views. There is a letter still in existence, in the handwriting of Cotton, addressed to the bishop, in which Cotton asks for further time to consider the points at issue, "inasmuch as his forbearance of the ceremonies was not from wilful refusal of conformity but from some doubt of judgment and from some scruple in conscience". Cotton now knew that either he had to make a stand and face trial or else he had to flee the country. In this matter he took advice from many friends. John Dod, the Puritan minister of Fawsley, told him, "I am old Peter and therefore must stand still and bear the brunt, but you, being young Peter, may go whither you will." Cotton was now taken seriously ill, and on 8th July, 1633, he resigned his living as Vicar of Boston parish church, seeing, as he said, "that neither his bodily health nor peace of the Church would now stand with his continuance there".

Flight to Massachusetts

His resignation was followed by the issue of writs for dealing with him in the courts, and it was now imperative that he leave the country at once. Travelling in disguise, he made his way to London, where John Davenport, the vicar of St. Stephen's, concealed him, till he could get away to New England which he reached on 4th September, 1633. He was not a young man who could more easily cope with his changing circumstances. Yet though forty-eight at the time, with a pastorate of twenty years behind him, he did not flinch for the sake of the truth to abandon all he had of home and friends, to go to New England.

On 10th October of the year he arrived he was solemnly appointed to work with John Wilson as co-pastor of the church at Boston, New England. Here he laboured for another nineteen years, dying in 1652 at the age of sixty-seven. It was men of such calibre that formed the backbone of the New England Colonies, ministers of the gospel who had given up all for the sake of the truth, who knew why they had done it. John Cotton stands out foremost as one of the great, godly men of the New England Colonies.

John Wilson

John Wilson, with whom John Cotton was co-pastor, had been educated at King's College, Cambridge, and was the son of a clergyman in the Church of England. At first he had been strongly prejudiced against the Puritans, but on reading a book of Richard Rogers, *Seven Treatises*, he was so blessed that he went to Wethersfield to hear the author, a godly Puritan, preach, and from that time his mind was completely changed. Now he joined their company and held prayer meetings in his rooms at Cambridge with the Puritans. Soon he came under the censure of the bishop and to avoid trouble his father sent him to the Inns of Court in London to study Law. But his mind was set on the ministry of the gospel and eventually he returned to Cambridge and entered Emmanuel College, the principal college of the Puritans. On leaving Emmanuel he became chaplain to Lady Scudamore, but having rebuked her guests one Sunday for talking about nothing but hawks and hounds after the morning sermon, he was asked to leave her service. Later he went to Sudbury to succeed an aged Puritan in the ministry there, but was continually harassed by the bishops and finally decided to make common cause with his neighbour John Winthrop of Groton, and sail for New England, which he did in 1630.

Zachariah Symmes and Peter Bulkely

While Wilson and Cotton were ministering in Boston, across the river in Charlestown Zachariah

Symmes was preaching the gospel. He had been minister at the Priory Church of Dunstable in Bedfordshire, but having been harassed by the church authorities, he had resigned his charge at Dunstable and come over to New England with Peter Bulkely. The latter had been the founder of the settlement at Concord (famous in the American War of Independence). Bulkely also was from Bedfordshire, where he had succeeded his father as rector of Odell on the Ouse. He was a man closely connected with the leaders of the parliamentary side in the Civil War. His brother-in-law was Oliver St. John, whose wife was a cousin of Oliver Cromwell. He had come out to New England with £6,000, a considerable fortune in those times, and making his way "through unknown woods" he had purchased from the Indians the land on the banks of the River Merrimac, and so become the founder and first minister of the town of Concord.

Richard, Increase and Cotton Mather

Dorchester, a few miles away from Boston, had Richard Mather as its minister. He had been Vicar for fifteen years at Toxteth near Liverpool, but had been suspended in 1633 for not using certain ceremonies of the Church of England. He had emigrated to New England and spent the remainder of his life ministering to his congregation at Dorchester (New England). His son Increase Mather was one of the presidents of Harvard College, and his grandson, in his *Magnalia Christi Americana,* collected together all the ecclesiastical records of the colony during the first eighty years of its history.

Samuel Whiting

To the north of Boston, New England, in the town of Lynn was a native of Boston in the home country. This was Samuel Whiting, whose father had once been Mayor of the town. Whiting had been to Emmanuel College, Cambridge, and after leaving it had first been chaplain to Sir Nathaniel Bacon and then assistant to Price, the vicar of King's Lynn. He had been cited before the Bishop of Norwich for not using some of the Anglican ceremonies and called to appear before the Court of High Commission in London.

Through the death of James I the legal proceedings were dropped for a time and then, through the intervention of the Earl of Lincoln, the matter was allowed to rest on the understanding that Whiting left the diocese of Norwich. He preached for the next seven or eight years at Skirbeck near his home town. Legal proceedings were however renewed against him and he left for New England in 1636. Preaching soon after his arrival there he said, "We in this country have left our near and our dear friends, but if we can get nearer to God here, He will be instead of all and more than all to us. He hath all the fulness of all the sweetest relations bound up in Himself, and we may take out of Him that which we forsook in friends near and dear to us as our own soul."

Thomas Shepard

Among the early authors of New England and one whose ministry was made a great blessing in the colony, was Thomas Shepard of Cambridge (New England). He had been a native of Towcester in Northamptonshire and, like so many of his Puritan contemporaries, had studied at Emmanuel College, Cambridge. After graduating he became preacher at Earls Colne in Essex where his ministry was singularly blessed, so that it was said of him when he went to America, that those who had been called under his ministry afterwards "went a thousand leagues to enjoy his ministry", in other words followed him to New England.

While in Essex he had been in the diocese of Laud the Bishop of London who had summoned him to appear before him and answer for his Puritanism. While Shepard had kept calm, Laud raged at him till Shepard says, "The bishop looked as though blood would have gushed out of his face and did shake as if he had been haunted with a fit of ague." The outcome of the interview was that with dire threats Laud banned Shepard from preaching in his diocese or undertaking any of the functions of a clergyman. "So I went away," says Shepard, "and blessed be God, I may go to Him." It is not without note that this evil man Laud, who so abused the servants of God, came to a solemn death, being executed for his part in the unconstitutional proceedings of the government of Charles I, when a tyrannical government was set up and the country governed without Parliament for eleven years.

Travelling from place to place in other dioceses and suffering many hardships, Shepard at length made his way to New England, where he became pastor of a Church organised at Newtown, afterwards known as Cambridge, his congregation consisting largely of members of his former flock, who had followed him from Essex. Here he remained until his death in 1649. His ministry was greatly used of the Lord, and Cotton Mather says that one of the reasons for the establishment of Harvard College at Cambridge was that the students might be able to sit under the sound of his ministry. In England at the end of the 16th century William Perkins exercised a similar powerful ministry at Cambridge among the students, many of whom were blessed through his preaching and formed the next generation of Puritan preachers in the seventeenth century.

Shepard, who died at the early age of forty-four, was the author of a number of works, the best known of which is *The Parable of the Ten Virgins*. His ministry in New England lasted eight or nine years and was described as experimental and soul-searching. Shepard had passed through deep conviction of sin after a life of gambling, bad company, and drunkenness in his days at Cambridge University. After a period of nine months the Lord brought him into gospel liberty. Having therefore passed through a pathway similar to John Bunyan, he could preach from his heart of "the things he had handled of the Word of life".

John Eliot, missionary to the Indians.

Another minister of great eminence in the history of New England was John Eliot. Little is known about his early history except that he was a graduate of Cambridge University in 1622 and after that was for a time an assistant in a school run by Thomas Hooker at Little Baddow near Chelmsford in Essex. Writing of this period of his life at Little Baddow he says, "To this place I was called through the infinite riches of God's mercy in Christ Jesus to my poor soul, for here the Lord said unto my dead soul, 'Live!', and through the grace of God, I do live, and I shall live for ever. When I came to this blessed family, I then saw, as never before, the power of godliness in its lively vigour and efficacy."

Threatened with proceedings in the Ecclesiastical Courts he made his way over to New England in 1631 and after serving the Church in Boston in the absence of their minister John Wilson, he became the minister of Roxbury near Boston, where he stayed till his death in 1690 at the advanced age of eighty-six, after a period of nearly sixty years as their pastor.

His ministry to his own countrymen did not prevent him from seeking to bring the gospel to the Indian tribes who lived in the territory nearby. These poor people were degraded in their ignorance and, but for the work of the Holy Spirit of truth, were unreachable by the gospel. Eliot made many journeys into their territory, learnt their language and reduced it to a grammatical form. After some time he became able to preach to them in their own language. In 1651 sufficient people had been converted for him to form a small church. Then he translated the Bible into their own tongue, some copies of which still survive.

Increase Mather writing to a friend in Holland in 1687 stated that there were no fewer than six churches of baptized Indians and among the Indians themselves no fewer than twenty-four native preachers, in addition to four English preachers who could preach to them in their own tongue. The people thus blessed under Eliot became known as the "praying Indians". Writing in 1651 Eliot says, "One of our principal men, Wamporas, is dead. He made so gracious an end of his life, embraced death with such holy submission to the Lord ... One of his sayings was, 'God giveth us three mercies in this world: the first is health and strength, the second is food and clothes, the third is sickness and death.'" Eliot was peculiarly a man of prayer; his last words were, "I have lost everything; my understanding leaves me, my memory fails me, my utterance fails me, but I thank God my charity holds out still" (1 Cor. 13, 13).

These are but a few of the godly ministers of New England who went on to mould the new colony by the preaching of the gospel.

CHAPTER 11

Inland Expansion - Connecticut

Early settlers including John Harvard

Others who went out to New England and did so much to mould the new community included Peter Hobart, born at Hingham in Norfolk, who founded the other Hingham, where there stands the oldest meeting house in New England, Charles Chauncery from Ware in Hertfordshire, who was brought before Ecclesiastical Courts in the home country, before he eventually sought freedom in New England, Nathaniel and Ezekiel Rogers, sons of two well-known Puritans, John Fisk, John Avery, John Norton and Jonathan Burr; finally, but not least, John Harvard, who dying without an heir, gave his library and half his estate to endow the college which bears his name, from which has developed Harvard University.

Danger from the English Government

At the time this college was founded in 1636, the colony of Massachusetts was in danger from the Indians and the home government. As early as 1635 the King, Charles I, had announced his intention of placing the New England colonies under a governor appointed by himself. In 1637 another royal declaration was issued, and the liberties of Massachusetts and the other colonies might have been lost, had it not been for the development of trouble in Scotland, where the King and Archbishop Laud were trying to undo the work of Knox and the Reformation. In 1638 a strict order was sent out by the government of Charles I for the return of the Massachusetts Charter to London for replacement by a new one. By this time, however, serious unrest was developing in England which eventually resulted in the Civil War, and thus the royal order could be safely ignored.

Expansion to the Connecticut valley

As more and more land was allocated to the colonists, new settlers were forced to look further afield. News had already reached the Massachusetts colonists of the great Connecticut River valley. Agents had been sent to report back, and in 1636 there was a large migration a hundred miles to the westward of Massachusetts Bay. Families from Cambridge, Dorchester, Watertown and Roxbury in Massachusetts formed new settlements and Churches in the Connecticut River valley at Hartford, Windsor, Wethersfield and Springfield respectively.

Thomas Hooker of Hartford

The man who had most influence in directing this westward movement was Thomas Hooker, a native of Leicestershire and Fellow of Emmanuel College, Cambridge. He had settled as a minister in the Church of England at Chelmsford, Essex, and his work had been greatly blessed. Many had come from numerous parts of Essex to hear him preach. But because he refused to use some of the ceremonies of the Church of England, he had been forced to leave the church and had commenced a school at Little Baddow in Essex where John Eliot had worked with him. Here in the godly home of Hooker, Eliot had been greatly blessed in his soul. Hooker had suffered further persecution in England and had eventually gone to Holland. There, he had heard of some of his friends who had gone out to New England and, at their request, he decided to join them, eventually becoming one of the leaders in the migration to the Connecticut valley.

In June 1636, when the Connecticut River had become free from ice and the woodland meadows offered pasture, the Cambridge congregation, a hundred or more in number, led by Thomas Hooker, taking with them 160 of their cattle and sending their furniture and supplies by sea, made their way to the new settlement. It was a migration of churches rather than individuals, these first comers being followed within a year by 800 others living in Dorchester, Watertown and Roxbury who moved into the Connecticut valley to Windsor, Hartford and Wethersfield, Springfield being settled later on.

The Colony of Connecticut

In 1636 the municipal independence of these towns was recognised; in 1637 the colony advanced to representative government by a meeting of deputies or committees from the different towns, and in 1638 the three towns formally declared themselves a commonwealth, with a governor, six assistants and deputies, the governor and assistants to be elected annually by the whole body of freemen met in General Court for that purpose. In one part the constitution of Connecticut was more liberal than that of Massachusetts, the governor being the only person from whom Church membership was required. Otherwise all freemen who had been admitted by a majority of their township, and had taken the oath of loyalty to the commonwealth, had the right of voting for the deputies at the General Court of Election.

At the opening session of the General Court in 1638 Thomas Hooker preached a sermon in which he maintained that the foundation of authority lay in the free consent of the people, and that the choice of magistrates belonged to the people, who also had the right to define the limits of the power of such magistrates or rulers. This constitution of Connecticut bears more resemblance to the present constitution of the United States than any other of the thirteen New England colonies, combining freedom of speech and worship within a democratic framework in which all freemen had a right to vote irrespective of their religious beliefs, thus providing the foundation of religious toleration as we know it today.

Conflict with the Indians

But the establishment of these settlements in the Connecticut valley had one sad consequence; they brought the settlers inevitably into serious conflict with the Indian tribes in the area, for the new Connecticut colony was in fact an outpost of Englishmen, projecting into the territory of the powerful Pequot tribe. Trouble had occurred with this tribe in 1633 when they had murdered a group of English traders. Sassacus their chief had promised the government in Boston that he would hand over the murderers, but had never done so. In 1636 another attack on traders was made and a number were murdered, the result of which was that the Boston authorities sent Endicott and a body of men to burn the Indians' wigwams and sink their canoes. They then demanded that the murderers be handed over and when this was refused they attacked them, killing several and burning and destroying their corn.

The reprisals for this attack of Endicott came not on the colony of Massachusetts, but on the newly formed settlements of Connecticut. All through the winter of 1636-1637 they were attacked, men were killed going to work, one man was burnt alive, and Wethersfield was attacked, ten people being killed and others captured. The Connecticut people sought the help of their fellow colonists in Boston and Plymouth. They sent ninety men under the command of John Mason, who, one bright, moonlit night, surrounded the Pequot stronghold, blocked the gateways of its fortified village and set fire to the wigwams inside.

The awful result was that about 700 Indians, their wives and children, perished in the fire and the Pequot tribe was all but wiped out, with the loss of two colonists killed and fourteen wounded.

After this dreadful episode in May 1637 the Indians did not dare attack the white man for nearly forty years. In 1638 a conference was held at Hartford when the survivors of the Pequot tribe submitted to the English and were divided between the Mohican and Narragansett tribes. The Connecticut colony was now no longer isolated from the Massachusetts colony along the coast by an Indian tribe, but was brought into direct communication with fellow colonists from the mouth of the Connecticut River to Boston Bay. Now the Indian tribes were detached and hemmed in, and the way was prepared for the last wave of migration from the home country, which brought to an end the great Puritan exodus from England to America.

Emigrants 1637-1640

About June 1637, the last wave of Puritan emigrants reached Boston. The two most prominent men among them was Theophilus Eaton, a member of the Massachusetts Bay Company and John Davenport their minister. Davenport had been the minister of a Church in Coleman Street, London. His preaching had brought him to the notice of Laud, then Bishop of London (this was in 1628), and he was waiting for Laud to deprive him of his living. Writing to Lady Mary Vere about this time describing the troubles gathering around him, he said, "I am in God's hands not theirs; to whose good pleasure I do contentedly and cheerfully submit myself. If it be His will to have me laid aside as a broken vessel, His will be done."

In later years he wrote to the same lady explaining his position and said, "The truth is, I have not forsaken my ministry, nor resigned my place, much less departed from the Church (of England) but am only absent awhile, to wait upon God for the settling and quieting of things, for light to discern my way; being willing to lie and die in prison, if the cause may be advantaged by it; but choosing rather to preserve the liberty of my person and ministry for the service of the Church elsewhere ... The only cause of my present suffering is the alteration of my judgment in matters of conformity to the ceremonies established; whereby I cannot practise them as formerly I have done; wherein I do not censure those that do conform. I know that I did conform with as much inward peace as now I do forbear; in both my uprightness was the same, but my light different. In this action I walk by that light which shineth unto me."

From 1634 to 1637 Davenport was in Holland, but in 1637 government spies reported that he had been seen at Braintree in Essex and in Hackney dressed like a country gentleman. The next that is heard of Davenport is that in June 1637 he had arrived at Boston, New England in the ship the *Hector*. Together with his friend Theophilus Eaton he spent some months searching for a good site for the new settlement. This they found at Quinnipack, on Long

Island Sound, where they made two successive purchases of land extending eight miles north-east and five miles south-west of the river and running ten miles inland. In this way the town of New Haven came to be founded in the spring of 1638.

In the next year, 1639, two other parties of emigrants, each forty in number, and each, like New Haven, joined together as an independent Church, settled at Guildford and Milford, both settlements placed on land purchased from the Indians. In 1640 Stamford on the mainland was added to the group and in 1643 the four towns were made to constitute the republic of New Haven, to which Southold on the western side of Long Island, and Branford were later added.

The end of the Puritan exodus

With the recall of Parliament in 1640 and the eventual downfall of Archbishop Laud, the reason for the Puritan exodus ceased and the exodus itself came to an end. Since the arrival of the *Mayflower* in 1620 the population had grown to 26,000. After 1640 for more than a century there was no considerable migration to this part of North America. These twenty years 1620-1640 constitute the formative period of New England history, and in a measure of the United States. "Had the emigration not started when it did, the solid and godly element there is in American life would not have been what it is. On the other hand, had that emigration continued longer, had England been depleted to exhaustion of her noblest blood, as

France was when her Huguenots (Protestants) were banished or slain, England's great struggle for constitutional freedom in the seventeenth century might have ended other than it did". (*The Pilgrim Fathers of New England*. John Brown. Pages 311-312).

It is interesting to note that at one time Oliver Cromwell considered leaving England for the New England colonies, but eventually felt led to stay to lead Parliament in its fight against royal absolutism. It is clear that, as Davenport saw the situation in his letter to Lady Mary Vere, some were called to go and others to stay. As in the sixteenth century at the time of the Reformation, some stayed to die at the stake, while others such as John Knox were led to flee to Europe.

It is also interesting to note today, in the last forty-five years, 1955 - 2000, there has been a remarkable burst of republication, independently, in both Britain and the United States, of the works of our godly Puritan forebears. How interested the Puritan settlers would have been to know that 350 years later they were not forgotten, and many of the books they loved to read were once again appearing in print in the home country and in the land of their exile.

CHAPTER 12

Growing Together

The colonies move toward union

Having followed the development of the colonies around Massachusetts Bay and the Connecticut valley over the period 1628 to 1643, it now remains for us to follow the progress of Plymouth colony in the same years, until the signing of the first Federal Union between the three colonies on 19th May 1643; then to follow the progress of the colonies until 1692, when they became a Crown colony under King William and Queen Mary; leading within the next hundred years to the Declaration of Independence in 1776 and the creation of the independent country, the United States of America.

Plymouth Colony 1628 - 1643

Since the year 1627, when De Rassières paid his visit to Plymouth colony, the settlers seem to have prospered steadily. In 1632 they held a thanksgiving day, on which they rejoiced "in an especial manner"; this too in spite of "a plague of mosquitoes and rattlesnakes". The colony was already beginning to spread beyond its boundaries, for as cattle increased people moved farther and farther in search of grassland. At first these visits were only for the summer, but eventually they led to the building of houses where they could spend the winter. Governor Bradford was very grieved at this movement away from the parent colony. In 1632 permission was granted for the organisation of a church for the families who had moved five miles to the north, and Elder Brewster was given the oversight of it. When the governor and his deputies gave this permission, they insisted that every man in this new settlement should be armed, being so far away from the fort on Burial Hill. Additionally these settlers had strong fences erected around their homes for extra protection.

The name of the new settlement was Duxbury, so called after Miles Standish's ancestral home in England, Duxbury Hall, near Chorley, Lancashire. For the sake of more fertile land several of the leading men migrated from Plymouth. They included Miles Standish, John Alden and William Brewster. A column stands on a hill near Duxbury in memory of Miles Standish. William Brewster's home there was called "Eagle's Nest", after a tall clump of whitewood trees which stood near it.

Others who had come from London left behind them in Duxbury such names as Billingsgate, Houndsditch and Blackfriars Brook. Edward Winslow obtained possession of land even beyond Duxbury, at a place known afterwards as Marshfield, though as he was governor of Plymouth colony in 1644, he does not seem to have severed his connection with it. So of the men who signed the *Compact* on board the *Mayflower* Miles Standish, William Brewster, John Alden, John Howland, George Soule and Henry Sampson all migrated to Duxbury, together with some who came later, including Jonathan Brewster, William Collier and Thomas Prince.

Governor Bradford found these inevitable changes hard to accept, but reluctantly gave the new settlement at Duxbury the rights of a self-governing town. After the incorporation of the town of Duxbury there followed the settlement of its first minister, Ralph Partridge. Marshfield was the next church organised, which was followed by settlements at Scituate, Barnstable, Taunton, Yarmouth and Sandwich, so that at the time that Plymouth entered the New England Confederacy it consisted of eight separate towns.

Relations with Massachusetts Colony

The relations between the settlers in Plymouth colony and those of Massachusetts Bay were good. John Cotton, in his farewell sermon at Southampton to John Winthrop and his company as they left the home country in March 1630, urged them to take the advice of those at Plymouth and do nothing to offend them. In 1628 when Endicott had arrived in New England with his party in a very sick condition Governor Bradford had quickly sent over his doctor, Samuel

Fuller, to help the new immigrants, and this had resulted in a firm union between Plymouth colony and Massachusetts settlement. At a later time, when there was great illness among the Massachusetts people, the colonists at Plymouth at their request had observed the same day for prayer and fasting on their behalf.

As the Massachusetts colony grew in numbers, governor Bradford rejoiced with them, pointing out "how of small beginnings great things have been produced by His hand that made all things of nothing and gives being to all things that are; and as one small candle may light a thousand, so the light here kindled hath shone to many, yea, in some sort to our whole nation. Let the glorious name of Jehovah have all the praise." During the years between 1630 and 1643 letters of friendship were exchanged and visits paid. In 1629 Governor Bradford and his friends went over to the ordination service at Salem; and the week after the arrival of Margaret Winthrop, Bradford paid a visit of congratulation to "his much honoured and beloved friend" her husband, the governor of Massachusetts. John Winthrop returned the kindness by lending the people of Plymouth twenty-eight pounds of gunpowder, when theirs had proved unusable.

In September 1632 Winthrop and his pastor John Wilson went over to Plymouth, walking the twenty-five miles from Wessagusset; and as towards evening they were nearing the town "the governor, William Bradford (a very discreet and grave man) met them and conducted them to the Governor's house where they very kindly entertained and feasted every day at several houses. On the Lord's day there was the Lord's Supper which they did partake in; and in the afternoon, Mr. Roger Williams, according to their custom, propounded a question, to which the pastor Mr. Smith spake briefly; then Mr. Williams preached; and after, the governor of Plymouth spake to the question; after him, Elder Brewster; then some two or three men of the congregation. Then Elder Brewster desired the governor of Massachusetts and Mr Wilson to speak to it ,which they did. When this was ended the deacon, Mr. Fuller, put the congregation in mind of their duty of contribution; whereupon the governor and all the rest went down to the deacon's seat and put money into the box and then returned."

There were thus some memorable men at this old world Sabbath worship, John Winthrop, William Bradford, William Brewster and Roger Williams. The following Wednesday, "as early as five in the morning, the Governor and his company came out of Plymouth, the Governor of Plymouth with the pastor Ralph Smith, and Elder Brewster accompanying them near half a mile out of the town in the dark". Some of the party went with them as far as the great Pembroke Swamp, ten miles from Plymouth. "When they came to the great river they were carried over by Luddam, their guide (as they had been when they came, the stream being very strong and deep), so governor Winthrop called that passage Luddam's Ford." (Winthrop. *Life and Letters,* ii. 105, 106).

Connections between the two colonies

The friendship which thus existed between the two colonies began to take a closer and more definite form. This was brought about by various factors, one being the danger from Indian tribes inland from the colonies; another the competition from French colonists to the north (the Quebec area of modern Canada) and the Dutch to the south (the area around present day New York). Also another factor was the many things which the colonists had in common, such as their English nationality, the reasons for their migration to North America, especially their union in the gospel which overrode their differences of government and Church order.

Articles of Confederation

Winthrop says that the first time the matter of a confederation was discussed was after the defeat of the Pequot tribe when magistrates and ministers of Connecticut met in Boston informally, and the matter was reported to the government of Plymouth colony. In 1638 a scheme of union was proposed by Massachusetts and rejected by Connecticut, the point of difference being whether the vote of a majority of Federal commissioners should be binding on each of the colonies. For about three years nothing further happened until the matter was raised again in 1642.

This resulted in a meeting of commissioners from Massachusetts, Connecticut and Plymouth in Boston in May 1643. After two or three conferences *Articles of Confederation* were agreed and eventually signed by all three colonies. Governor Bradford in his history has given the eleven *Articles* in full. The preamble states that all the colonies came to America with the same end and aim, that is, to advance the kingdom of our Lord Jesus Christ, and to enjoy the liberties of the gospel in purity with peace; and living as they do, encompassed with people of several nations and strange languages, they conceive it their bounden duty without delay to enter into a present association for mutual help and strength.

The confederation thus to be formed was to be called *The United Colonies of New England*, and to constitute a league of friendship for offence and defence, mutual advice and help upon all just occasions, both for preserving and propagating the truth and liberties of the gospel, and for mutual safety and welfare. Each colony was to preserve its own government; all public charges were to be met by contributions levied on the colonies in proportion to the number of their inhabitants; the affairs of the confederation were to be managed by commissioners, two from each colony, all being of good standing as church members; the annual meetings were to be held in the colonies in rotation, Massachusetts having two turns in succession.

Since all power of taxation, except for a common levy, was left to the individual colonies, and the board of commissioners had but little governing power, and was rather more like a consulting body, the confederation was rather more of a treaty of friendship than a union of colonies. It is still however important as being the first experiment in the direction of one government for all the colonies. One source of difficulty lay in the fact that Massachusetts had a population of about 15,000, whereas Connecticut and Plymouth numbered about 3,000 each.

Massachusetts had therefore to provide the largest amount of money and men in time of conflict and thus might expect to have the greatest say in the decisions that were made. Also there was the difficulty of church membership being essential for a vote in Massachusetts but not in Plymouth colony. It would appear to colonists in Plymouth that if the confederation came about they might lose some of their freedom and some people, not church members, might lose their vote. For the colonists in Plymouth, what they lost in liberty, they would gain in security and commercial progress. It was inevitable that in union with the other colonies, Plymouth was bound in time to lose its own self-reliance and become gradually swallowed up in the United colonies. The union however worked well as a means of concentrating military strength and paved the way in the following century for the development of the American people into a nation.

The United Colonies

The commissioners who met in Boston to form the union of states paid little attention to what the English Government might think of their action. In England in 1643 all was confusion in the Civil War and neither side was in any position to take serious note of what was happening across the Atlantic in America. It was on 19th May, 1643 that the delegates of the colonies met at Boston to sign the *Articles of the Confederation.*

Death of William Brewster

The greatest man among the founders of the Plymouth Plantation did not live to see that day. A month earlier on 10th April, "to the great sadness and mourning of them all", William Brewster passed peacefully away. With deep sorrow his friend governor Bradford, recording the fact, described him as "my dear and loving friend; a man that hath done and suffered much for the Lord Jesus and the gospel's sake; and had borne his part in the weal and woe with this poor persecuted church above thirty-six years in England, Holland, and in this wilderness, and done the Lord and them faithful service in his place and calling."

In Bradford's life history of Brewster from his days at Scrooby Manor House to his home at "Eagle's Nest," we hear how bravely in times of great stress this godly man was enabled to stand firm and bear his part of the burden with the rest. Bradford says that on more than one occasion Brewster had lived for many months without bread or corn having many times nothing but fish. "Yet he lived," says Bradford, "by the blessing of God, in health until very old age, and would labour with his hands in the fields as long as he was able. And when the church had no other minister, he taught twice every Sabbath, and that both powerfully and profitably, to the great contentment of the hearers and their comfortable edification. Yea, many were brought to God by his ministry. He did more in their behalf in a year than many that have their hundreds a year do in all their lives."

William Bradford further describes the character of the man he had known since his own days at Austerfield: "He was wise and discreet and well-spoken, having a grave deliberate utterance; of a very cheerful spirit, very sociable and pleasant among his friends, of an humble and honest mind; of a peaceable disposition, undervaluing himself and his own abilities and sometimes overvaluing others; inoffensive and innocent in his life and conversation, which gained him the love of those without as well as those within. Yet he would tell them plainly of their faults and evils, both publicly and privately, but in such a manner as usually was well taken from him ... In teaching he was very stirring and moving the affections, also very plain and distinct in what he taught, by which means he became the more profitable to the hearers. He had a singular gift in prayer, both public and private, in ripping up the heart and conscience before God, in the humble confession of sin and begging the mercies of God in Christ for the pardon thereof. He always thought it was better for ministers to pray oftener, and divide their prayers, than to be too long and tedious in the same, except upon solemn and special occasions, as on days of humiliation and the like."

Bradford, describing Brewster's end says, "He was near fourscore years of age when he died. He had this blessing added by the Lord to all the rest, to die in his bed in peace among the midst of his friends, who mourned and wept over him, and ministered what help and comfort they could unto him, and he again re-comforted them whilst he could. His sickness was not long. Until the last day thereof he did not wholly keep his bed. His speech continued until somewhat more than half a day before his death, and then failed him; and about nine or ten of the o'clock that evening he died, without any pang at all. A few hours before he drew his breath short, and some few minutes before his last he drew his breath long, as a man fallen into a sound sleep without any pangs or gaspings, and so sweetly departed this life into a better."

Death of many of the Pilgrim Fathers.

Six years after the death of William Brewster, John Winthrop died and the inhabitants of Massachusetts laid him "with great solemnity and honour in the grave" in the burial ground of King's Chapel in Boston city. It was said of him that "his epitaph was engraven in the minds of the people, as a worthy gentleman who had done good in Israel, having spent not only his whole estate, but his bodily strength and life in the service of the country, as a burning torch spending his health and wealth for the good of others".

His death was in 1649. In 1652 John Cotton passed away, while Edward Winslow, Miles Standish and William Bradford died in 1655, 1656 and 1657 respectively. To William Bradford, the great historian of the Plymouth colony, posterity owes a deep debt of gratitude for his simple and poignant account of the sufferings and endurance of the Pilgrim Fathers.

While one generation was passing away and another was taking its place the older generation had not forgotten to sow some of the seeds of learning which they themselves had acquired at the two great seats of learning, Oxford and Cambridge in the home country. Thus in 1636 the General Court of Massachusetts voted £400, a sum equivalent to the whole taxation of the colony, to found a college or grammar school. In the following year, John Harvard, a graduate of Emmanuel College, Cambridge, gave the college £700 and his library of 260 books.

In 1642 the college was placed under the control of a board of governors consisting of the governor of Massachusetts, his deputy, his assistants and six ministers of nearby towns, and a president of the college was appointed. In 1650 the college was further endowed with the proceeds of the tolls taken at the ferry boat between Charlestown and Boston. Thus the foundations were laid of Harvard University, whose influence was felt by all the colonies.

Connecticut soon followed the example of Massachusetts by opening a college at Saybrook which, afterwards at New Haven, grew to the great University of Yale. These two places of learning were the forerunners of many other colleges and universities in the United States. Thus the first generation of settlers showed the value they placed on education.

In 1647 the General Court of Massachusetts established elementary schools in settlements where there were up to fifty households, and grammar schools where there were a hundred households. In Plymouth Colony in 1662 the governing body laid down that each town should have a schoolmaster, and in 1670 they offered financial help to any town which would set up a free school of elementary and grammar school level. Plymouth itself was the first town to do this.

The New England Colonies 1643 - 1692

From 1643, for the next twenty-one years the New England Colonies governed themselves in full independence. After the Restoration of Charles II to the English throne in 1664 however, interference returned from the home country. In that year a commission was sent out to administer and inspect the colonies and was charged to secure the King's rights. It was to examine the trade laws (known as the Navigation Acts), examine the state of religion, the administration of justice, the treatment of native Indians, the system of education, and had also certain secret diplomatic powers. But it made little impression on the colonists who seem to have been able to resist such interference quietly, and all it left was a feeling of bitterness towards the restored monarchy and its pretence to govern the colonies.

The next event of importance in the history of the colonies was ten years later in 1674, when a disastrous war broke out with the Indians. The horrors of this war were enormous. Out of ninety towns in the colonies, twelve were utterly destroyed, while a further forty were the scene of fire and slaughter. One in every twelve men of military age was killed as well as large numbers of women and children. Nearly every household in the colonies was in mourning and the cost of the war was so great that in 1676 the direct taxation in Massachusetts was sixteen times the normal amount. In Plymouth the cost of the war was equally great.

For the Indians it meant that they were driven out of the coastal areas for ever, and they suffered a huge loss of life, only returning occasionally from the interior of the continent to which they had been driven, to make sporadic attacks on the western frontier of the United Colonies. It was a sad collision and one which the early colonists had foreseen and constantly expressed a wish to avoid; in fact their great object had been to bring the gospel to the Indians. After all America was the rightful homeland of the Indian tribes and the Pilgrim Fathers were invaders, driven from their own land by religious persecution. Now the Indians in the colonial area were entirely removed and the red man disappeared from the history of the United Colonies into the interior. It makes sad and solemn reading, after the work of such men as John Eliot, the godly minister to the Indians.

In 1684 came the long expected intervention by the British Government. In June the Charter of Massachusetts was withdrawn and King James II claimed the colony as royal property. This was followed by the harsh government of Sir Edmund Andros from 1685 to 1688. The Glorious Revolution of 1688 in England overthrew James II, the Catholic monarch, and brought William of Orange from Holland and his wife Queen Mary to the English throne to preserve the Protestant Constitution. While this event removed Andros, at the same time it put an end to the old colonial government. In 1692 governor Phipps was appointed by the Crown. He came over with a new Charter which united Massachusetts Bay, Plymouth colony, and other territory stretching from Martha's Vineyard to the Gulf of the River St. Lawrence into one royal province of Massachusetts. From that year, 1692, the government created by the Pilgrim Fathers in Plymouth colony ceased to exist and a new chapter opened up in American history with the establishment of a Crown colony under an English governor which ended with the Declaration of Independence in 1776 and the creation of the United States of America.

Bibliography

Primary Sources.

The Great Works of Christ   Banner of Truth
in America, by Cotton Mather   Trust 1979

Chronicles of the Pilgrim Fathers   Everyman's Library
[Includes *The New England Memorial*   1936
by Nathaniel Morton and Edward Winslow's
Relation.]

Journal of William Bradford   New York 1906
Edited by W.T. Davis   London 1909

Journal of John Winthrop   New York 1908
Edited by J.K. Hosmer

Secondary Sources

The Pilgrim Fathers of New England   London 1920
by John Brown B.A. D.D.

The Mayflower Pilgrims and their Pastor   Worthing 1970
by D.G. Fountain M. A.

The Mayflower Pilgrims   South Carolina
by Dr David Beale   and Belfast 2000